Moneymaking
MOMS

Moneymaking
MOMS

How Work at Home Can Work for You

Caroline Hull and Tanya Wallace

A Citadel Press Book
Published by Carol Publishing Group

To my children, Christopher, Jonathan, Emma, Lucy, and Anna, my inspiration, my teachers...my friends. Thank you. Love, Mum.

To my daughters, Ashley Jordan, Abby Taylor, and Allie McKenna Wallace, with love, my sole reason for entering the world of home-based business and my daily inspiration.

Carol Publishing Group edition, 1999

A Citadel Press Book
Published by Carol Publishing Group
Citadel Press is a registered trademark of Carol Communications, Inc.

Editorial, sales and distribution, rights and permissions inquiries should be addressed to Carol Publishing Group, 120 Enterprise Avenue, Secaucus, N.J. 07094

In Canada: Canadian Manda Group, One Atlantic Avenue, Suite 105, Toronto, Ontario M6K 3E7

Carol Publishing Group books may be purchased in bulk at special discounts for sales promotions, fund-raising, or educational purposes. Special editions can be created to specifications. For details, contact Special Sales Department, Carol Publishing Group, 120 Enterprise Avenue, Secaucus, N.J. 07094

Manufactured in the United States of America
10 9 8 7 6 5 4 3 2

Library of Congress Cataloging-in-Publication Data

Hull, Caroline.
   Moneymaking moms : how work at home can work for you / Caroline Hull and Tanya Wallace.
      p.   cm.
   "A Citadel Press book".
   Includes index.
   ISBN 0—8065—1993–2 (pbk.)
1. Home-based businesses—United States. 2. Working mothers–
United States. 3. Self-employed women—United States. 4. Work and family—United States. I. Wallace, Tanya. II. Title.
HD2336.U5H86
658'.041—dc21   98-10383
                                                                              CIP

Contents

Preface

The kids are in bed, the toys put away or at least shoved discreetly into a corner of the room, and as you listen to the soft swish of yet another load of laundry in the rinse cycle, you have miraculously found a moment to open this book.

Every woman who becomes a mother almost instantly develops a newfound respect for a role that most of us have always taken for granted. How many of you have felt an overwhelming urge to call your own mothers and ask, "Why didn't you tell me?" And then, almost as an afterthought, thank her for all she did, because now you know! Motherhood is a special club with no laminated membership cards, no secret handshakes, no annual conventions to faraway resorts, but once you belong to it, you are members for life. You share in all the secrets that it possesses—the joys, the pains, the pride, the anxiety, the unbreakable bond between mother and child.

It is amazing how much time a new mother can spend worrying about the sudden responsibilities that go with the job—how such a little bundle can add so much weight to your shoulders. Some things, like the huge task of having and raising children, never change; the world around us, however, does. You are faced with higher prices, higher taxes, and incomes that have not kept pace with your way of life. Many families deal with this by relying on two incomes. Both parents work, the bills are paid, the house is furnished, and annual vacations are possible.

There's just one problem: Who's watching the kids? So many parents who are faced with putting their babies in day care in order to achieve their financial goals have found that the price they pay is far too high. If you currently work outside the home, fill out the worksheet called "How Much Does Your Job Cost You?" (on page 5) and discover, after all is said and done, how much you really make.

More and more mothers (and fathers—if your husband is the stay-at-home working parent, he will enjoy this book!) are working their way back home by putting their talents to work. Building businesses based on their knowledge, experience, and what they enjoy, moms are finding that they can combine the very real and demanding world of motherhood with the challenging and exciting world of business, replacing and often exceeding their former adjusted incomes.

The secret is slowly getting out. You can be home with your children, sharing and shaping their daily lives, and *still* contribute significantly to your family's income. But there's no doubt that attempting to combine home-based work with parenting responsibilities is a challenging—sometimes overwhelming—task that requires strength, perseverance, determination, and a well-developed sense of humor!

Moneymaking Moms: How Work at Home Can Work for You will take you on a step-by-step guided tour of starting and succeeding in your home-based business. It will lead you through the process of selecting a business that is right for you and your home life. It will give you the strategies you need to build and promote your business. You will learn how you can start your business on a shoestring budget and how to market your product or service efficiently and cost-effectively. You will even learn how to include your family in your business in order to keep them involved and excited about each new hurdle you clear. You will also be providing a wonderful role model for your children as they watch you build your business from home. Tanya's daughters, for example, put together a lemonade stand one summer. When asked where her four-year-old sister was, the seven-year-old promptly responded, "She's out marketing." The apple does not fall far...

Regard this book as a teacher and friend, be comfortable with it, use it, write in it, refer to it, and learn from it. *Moneymaking Moms* is written especially for mothers. Unlike other home-based business how-to guides, *Moneymaking Moms* addresses the very real concerns of mothers struggling to find and maintain a comfortable balance between working and tending to the needs of a growing family. Do not tuck it away in a cupboard or drawer; keep it close by and read it often. It will become your best resource.

As authors of *Moneymaking Moms* we know what you will face on a day-to-day basis. We've been there. With eight children between us (five of whom were under the age of eight at the time this book was conceived) and over ten years of experience in combining children and business, we are sure to address all your concerns about working from home. There were times in both our careers as home-based "business moms" that we questioned and wrestled with the choices we had made.

You, too, will experience and come to terms with the challenge of wearing the multiple hats of home-based mom, entrepreneur, wife, and friend. You will worry when your business line doesn't ring enough; you will worry when it rings too often. You will wonder if you are giving your family enough time and attention and if you are giving your business enough of the same. You will bask in the glory of your finest business accomplishments and kick yourself a hundred times when you make a mistake. You will congratulate yourself for a job well done and in the very next moment panic as you wonder if you'll be in business next year or even next week. It's all part of the process.

But as you stop to hug your little ones, take a break to curl up in a comfortable chair and read a story, or play a favorite game together, you will have no doubt that it is absolutely worth the time, work, and attention that your business demands. You will never again have to call your boss, stammering excuses because your child is running a fever and you need to stay home with him. Caroline spent an entire month playing Florence Nightingale as all four of her children came down with chicken pox one after the other. But she was able to continue working in between giving oatmeal baths, applying calamine lotion, and furnishing much-needed hugs. Few bosses would have tolerated such a situation.

If you dream of being home with your children, then home is where you should be. If you need additional income to make that dream come true, you have taken the first step by opening this book. It *can* happen, and it will. Your determination and perseverance can help you grow a healthy business as you raise a healthy and happy family.

And so we take you to Phase I. From mother to mother, good luck.

Using Our Checklists

One of the hardest things about working independently at home is dealing with the lack of praise and encouragement from peers and supervisors. There are no pats on the back or congratulations for a job well done; it's up to you to keep yourself encouraged and excited about your progress. Easier said than done, right?

We've included a checklist for each phase of *Moneymaking Moms* (you'll find them at the end of each phase in the book) so that you can check off the steps as you take them and see the progress you're making at a glance.

Phase I

Getting Started

This book is divided into three phases, each designed especially to help you build your business from the bottom up with a strong foundation and healthy structure. This first important phase takes you step-by-step through each stage of the process. In the pages that follow you will find information, help, and advice to assist you in choosing and launching a business that's right for you, establish an appropriate business identity, set up and equip your home office, and explore the various child-care options available to you. We also guide you through the more mundane but equally important aspects of starting a business, such as obtaining the necessary permits, licenses, insurance, and financing. Each of the three parts of the book is followed by a checklist to help you keep track of all the details you must attend to in that "phase" of the process.

Before you start, give some thought to what you expect your business to do for you and what you expect to do for it. Are you looking for a part-time outlet for your creative energies that you hope will bring in just enough money to cover the monthly car or orthodontia payments? Or do you see this as a first step toward your goal of building a highly profitable, growth-oriented business over the long term? *As long as your business meets your aspirations, then it is a success.* You'll read about both types of home-based business moms in this book.

Starting a business is not something that should be undertaken lightly. You will invest time, money, and effort into your new venture, so it's worth taking the time to set it up properly in the beginning. Phase I will show you how.

1

Your First Steps

You may never have given a second thought to staying home after you had your baby. Like many of us, you planned your return to work following a short maternity leave, assuming that life would continue much as before. So it may have come as quite a surprise when your new baby arrived and began to tug at your heartstrings, causing you to question so many of your earlier assumptions. Suddenly, home seems like an awfully good place to be.

Deciding to Stay Home

For many, the decision to stay home is made the moment the doctor hands you your new baby. Suddenly, nobody is good enough, trustworthy enough, smart enough, or caring enough to take care of your child. The position can be filled by one person and one person only: You. So you spend the next six weeks drafting your departure speech to your boss and fretting over how you will make ends meet.

Or it may have been that defining moment when you left the day from hell at work and were greeted by an even unfriendlier day at home: laundry piled high, sick kids, an empty fridge, and the fact that the fourth baby-sitter in three months has quit.

Or it may have been simply losing touch with your family, feeling that you were all missing out on time together that can never be reclaimed—a feeling far worse than a lousy day at the office.

Whatever prompted your decision, you are about to journey into the world of the home-based business mom. What a journey it will be. You will leave the safe haven of your corner office or cubicle and report each morning instead to the demands of little ones in seemingly continuous need of juice, crackers, and Barney.

As you make your way, you must believe in yourself and your abilities. You must be prepared to be your own boss, your best friend, your worst critic, and your biggest promoter. You must prepare yourself for the hardships that owning a home-based business will inflict, and most of all, you must have the support of your family and friends.

Surround yourself with others who are positive and enthusiastic about the exciting decision you have made. If your spouse is ambivalent or downright negative about the idea, start by figuring out how much your job costs you (see page 5). Sharing the results with him will provide a starting point for more discussion.

Of course, it is very comfortable to receive a paycheck twice a month, and for some couples losing a significant portion of the household income will require major adjustments in lifestyle, spending habits, and expectations. But you may be pleasantly surprised at how little you really must recover.

Can You Afford to Stay Home? Can You Afford Not To?

Sarah Miller's parents wake her each day at 5:00 A.M. She eats breakfast, and is dressed and ready by 6:00 A.M. to begin her commute to the place where she will spend the next twelve hours or so. She has become accustomed to her setting, sees new faces each day, and takes comfort in seeing a few regulars here and there. At 6:00 P.M., Sarah begins her commute home, and by 8:00 P.M. her evening has been consumed by dinner, a bath, and some time with her family. By 8:10 P.M., it is off to bed. After all, four-month-old infants need their rest, and the process must be repeated again tomorrow. Many evenings Sarah's parents gaze at their sleeping child and wonder what her day was like.

Surprised? Don't be. Sarah is just one of countless infants across the United States who repeat that routine daily. Although it is a schedule unappealing to most grown-ups, Sarah knows nothing else and therefore has no option but to adapt to the repetitiveness.

We live in a society in which it has become acceptable to separate infants from their parents for long hours each day. In many cases children begin as early as six weeks of age, spending more time in a day-care setting, away from their parents, than they spend in their own homes. Although many day-care providers give a child a warm and loving environment, many more are poorly staffed and equipped and find it difficult to attend to each child's individual needs. It is too early to tell how this will affect our children long term, but it is safe to say that there will be some who will simply fall through the cracks. An increasing number of parents are not prepared to take this risk.

For many, the thought of giving up their salary is very scary, and the thought of attempting to replace all or some of it is even scarier. Realistically, you will probably need to make certain trade-offs if you are leaving a well-paid position in order to stay home with your children. But it's surprising how much you can shave off your monthly budget by implementing a few simple lifestyle changes. For example, start *using* those coupons you've been clipping or make going to see a movie or out to dinner a special event rather than a weekly ritual. And don't forget just how much working outside the home can cost you. Complete the following work sheet, and you may be surprised at the additional expenses you incur just by going to work!

How Much Does Your Job Cost You?

1. How much do you spend each month for child care as a result of your working outside the home?
   _____ Multiply by 12 _____

2. How much do you spend on clothing for work each month?
_____ Multiply by 12 _____

3. How much do you spend each month for dry-cleaning your working wardrobe? _____ Multiply by 12 _____

4. How much do you spend daily for breakfast, lunch, and snacks as a result of working outside the home?
_____ Multiply by 240 _____

5. How much do you spend each week for parking?
_____ Multiply by 50 _____

6. Approximately how much do you spend each week in gas and car care or other transportation to get to and from work?
_____ Multiply by 50 _____

7. Add the totals together._____

Your job costs you _____/ year in after-tax money.

The Work/Kid Combo

Here's the good news:

- You may need to replace far less income than you think.

- You may be pleasantly surprised at how little some home-based businesses cost to set up.

- You can use the skills you've gained at your current job to build a business. You have the training; all you need now is to build a service out of it.

- You are free to build your business any way you like. Make it a product, a service, or both.

- You will be your children's primary caregiver and have the satisfaction of knowing that they are being cared for by the best candidate for the job—you.

- You will take part in your child's every accomplishment and be able to offer assistance each time he or she requires guidance or reassurance.

- You will thrill in your own accomplishments as your business begins to flourish.
- You will become quite educated in the building and managing of a small business. You will learn something new every day.
- You will meet new people and earn respect as a business owner and self-proclaimed entrepreneur.
- You will not have to face traffic, long commutes, and crabby bosses. You will work when you want to work—not when someone tells you to.
- You will see your children each and every day, sometimes all day.
- You will be your own boss.

Now the bad news:
- You will undoubtedly face an adjustment period as you escape the hustle-and-bustle business world and settle in at home.
- When your first business call comes in, you will at the same time be dealing with a screaming two-year old who is determined to get just one more cookie out of you.
- You will make mistakes that will cost you money. (The good news is that you will learn from those mistakes.)
- You will feel compelled to go above and beyond the call of duty to earn and keep the trust of each new client. (Not a bad thing at all, but it does require a lot of time and effort initially.)
- You will be the entire lifeline of your business, from answering the phone to opening the mail to marketing your trade. Its fate rests on your shoulders.
- You will find it difficult to meet the demands of both a growing family and a growing business.
- There are no coffee breaks, lunch breaks, office parties, or Christmas bonuses.
- When you leave for vacation, you rarely leave the office far behind. Thank goodness for calling cards, voice mail, faxes, and modems.
- You will see your children each and every day, sometimes all day.
- You will be your own boss.

Is a Home-Based Business Right for You?

Not every home-based business will succeed, but you can maximize
your chances of success if you are honest about your strengths and
weaknesses. Have a friend or relative help you answer the following
questions to evaluate your business for potential success!

1. I am a self-starter. I like to take the initiative rather than rely on
someone else to get me started.

true   somewhat true   not true

2. I like to work alone and without constant supervision; in fact I
do better when I supervise myself.

true   somewhat true   not true

3. I am very organized and manage my time well.

true   somewhat true   not true

4. I always like to work from a plan which I can review from time
to time to measure my progress.

true   somewhat true   not true

5. I am assertive and confident. I enjoy talking to people about
what I do.

true   somewhat true   not true

6. I have a positive and optimistic outlook. If I prepare myself
adequately, I believe I will be successful.

true   somewhat true   not true

7. I am responsible and trustworthy and prepared to be held
accountable for the things I do and say.

true   somewhat true   not true

8. I am extremely persistent. If I have made my mind up to do something, I will keep at it until I succeed.

     true   somewhat true   not true

9. I am resourceful and enjoy researching and exploring new areas and interests.

     true   somewhat true   not true

10. Although I don't like making mistakes, I see them as an opportunity to learn and do better next time.

     true   somewhat true   not true

11. I am energetic and have lots of stamina. I like to work hard and don't mind working long hours.

     true   somewhat true   not true

Obviously, the more "true" answers you marked, the more likely you are to do well in a home-based business.

If you have marked "somewhat true" frequently, you will probably have more difficulty, but work on improving your weaknesses and you can still succeed. You might also want to consider going into business with a partner whose personality strengths can complement your weaker areas.

If most of your answers were "not true," you will probably find going into business for yourself an uphill battle. Our advice is: Don't quit your day job!

The Telecommuting Option

You've done the math over and over, cut out all the extras, and pared your expenses to a minimum, but you *still* can't afford to give up your salary and benefits. Is there any way you can get back home? Maybe. You might be a candidate for telecommuting—provided your supervisor is open to the concept. Telecommuting simply means moving your job from the office to your home on a full- or part-time basis. You communicate with colleagues via telephone, fax, and modem and, depending on how often you work from home, attend regularly scheduled meetings at the office location.

Obviously, not all jobs lend themselves to this work style. Typically, jobs that require little face-to-face contact with others and depend heavily on a computer, telephone, and fax are good candidates for taking home. Additionally, not all personality types are suited to telecommuting. To telecommute successfully, you'll need to be relatively self-motivated and disciplined as well as enjoy working alone. So, if you want to give it a try, follow these steps and keep your fingers crossed:

- Develop a proposal justifying your request to telecommute and present it to your supervisor. Make sure you include information on where you plan to work, how you will set up your office, arrangements you will make for child care, and the hours you will be available. Also be prepared with facts and figures to back up your proposal—statistics that document productivity increases for people who work at home; savings to the company from freeing up your office, parking spaces, and equipment.

- Be prepared to invest in the necessary equipment yourself. If you already have a computer, you will need to add a modem and communications software as well as an additional telephone line and possibly a fax. Your assumption that you will provide the tools necessary to make the arrangement work will impress your manager and persuade him to give your proposal serious consideration.

- Sell it to co-workers, customers, and clients. Many telecommuters experience problems with co-workers who don't understand the nature of the arrangement. You're home. Must mean you're goofing off, right? Often telecommuting programs fall apart because supervisors get tired of complaints from other workers who feel that the telecommuter is getting "preferential treatment." Develop a strategy to keep in touch with colleagues and organize regular meetings where grievances can be aired and dealt with.

- Ask for a little before you ask for a lot. If telecommuting is rela-

---

Jobs Suited to Telecommuting

Accounting	Graphic design
Auditing	Research
Computer programming	Telephone sales, or other
Copywriting	telephone work
Data entry	Telemarketing
Desktop publishing	Translation
Editing	Travel reservations

---

tively unknown within your organization, ask to work from home just one or two days each week at first. Then, as your supervisors see results, they will be more kindly disposed to increasing your time at home.

■ Don't be surprised or discouraged if your first request is denied or ignored. Telecommuting, despite the media hullabaloo, is still a relatively unusual work option for most organizations. Although it makes sense in many environments, too many managers and supervisors are still skeptical that work can be done efficiently from a home office. Put your proposal on the back burner and your nose to the grindstone and bring it up again in a couple of months.

A Personal Glimpse   Delilah Ray began telecommuting shortly after the birth of her daughter, Vanessa: "When my daughter was born, I quickly realized that my original plan of going back to work full-time was not going to be feasible. I simply could not leave her, but my husband's salary was not enough to pay our bills. So I approached my boss about telecommuting."

Despite Delilah's reputation as a reliable, diligent worker who needed minimal supervision, and her agreeing to come into the office for meetings at least one day a week, her boss rejected her proposal to telecommute. Undaunted, Delilah approached other managers in the company and was thrilled when she was offered a transfer to another department under the terms she had requested. Delilah now revels in the advantages of her working arrangement: "I can easily work whether I am sick or my daughter is sick or the roads are icy. I earn money while being a full-time parent to my daughter. I have to commute an hour and a half only once a week instead of five days a week. I don't wear panty hose or high heels except to church on Sunday and one day a week. I put my feet on the desk while I type. I avoid the worst of office politics while still seeing co-workers in person once a week."

But she acknowledges some disadvantages: "Many colleagues at work make comments like 'Gee, I wish I only worked one day a week.' I am out of the loop on much of the office gossip, and obviously I am firmly established on the 'mommy track' and will not be getting a raise or promotion anytime soon, if ever."

However, the bottom line for Delilah is that she can be home with her daughter, continue to earn a salary, and feel good about her family-work mix. "I am the one caring for my daughter, and that is the most important thing to me, so all the sacrifices and downsides are worth it to us."

Husbands Are Family Too!

How does your husband feel about the possibility of your starting a new business venture? Is he excited, enthusiastic, supportive? Is he going to jump in and take up the slack while you spend time developing your business? Has he suggested realigning your shared household responsibilities to free up additional time for you to work? And is he prepared for the fact that you won't be quite as available to him or the family now that you have a business to run?

Or is he only going along with your venture provided you fit your business activities in around everything you already do?

Let's face it; your life as a business mom will be much easier if your husband happily agrees to reevaluate your individual roles within the family and willingly embraces any changes. Unfortunately, though, it isn't always that straightforward. Your husband may feel very ambivalent about your business venture and may need help to become the supportive, cheerleading partner you need.

The suggestions that follow should help all but the most stubbornly opposed spouse feel excited about your business and even partially responsible for its success:

- Discuss your day with your husband when he returns home. Keep him up-to-date as your business progresses and celebrate with him when you have reason. Let him know that his help and support are instrumental to your success.

- Make time every day for just the two of you— even if it's only fifteen minutes or so. If you rarely spend time together and he feels he is playing second fiddle to your business, he will become resentful.

- At least once a month go out to dinner at a favorite restaurant— again, just the two of you. If you are talking about business matters, let your business pick up the tab. Otherwise, use this time to catch up and enjoy one another's company while you enjoy a meal prepared by someone else. Throw in a bottle of your favorite wine or indulge in a yummy dessert and luxuriate in a well-deserved break.

- Prepare him in advance for any event that is going to take up more of your time than usual. For example, you may have an especially time consuming project coming up or you may want to sign up for a course at your local college that will benefit your business. Discuss it with him *before* you make a commitment. You'll need to make sure that *he* isn't about to embark on a particularly busy period at work. Coordinate your schedules so that together you can devise a plan to cope with your increased absences. Let him know that the situation is temporary and you will soon be back to your old schedule.

- Share the tough times. Let him know when you are overwhelmed, frustrated, or just dealing with a bad day in the office. Ask him for advice and listen when he offers it! He may have some constructive suggestions and will appreciate your confidence in his opinion.

The support of your spouse is really key to balancing your business and family life. If your husband is used to you being at home and taking care of all the household chores, he may be a little resistant to change. If you are giving up a substantial income to stay home with your baby, he may feel overburdened by the responsibility of supporting your family until your business starts to make money. Both responses are understandable, so prepare your spouse as well as you can before your business really gets rolling and keep the lines of communication open. He will appreciate it and so will you!

A Personal Glimpse Lora Davidek runs a business giving administrative and secretarial support to all kinds of clients scattered all over the country. She does "just about everything for them, including buying gifts, reminding them of birthdays and events, designing newsletters, sending monthly billing statements, etc." In fact, Lora does just about any project (within reason!) that comes up.

She has two sons, ages four-and-a-half years and 18 months, and became a work-at-home mom after her second son was born because she couldn't bear leaving them and hearing one more time, "Mommy, please stay home."

Although her husband has been generally supportive, there are times when he doesn't quite "get it."

"My husband is very supportive, but sometimes he doesn't understand that although I am home all day, I still do not have time to do laundry and housework or to do those little errands he can't find the time to do, since he works out of the home. Those little errands sometimes run me all day—especially taking two small children with me!"

The good news is that her husband contributes something quite significant to her business—and when she most needs it. "During those times when I yell, 'I should just go back to work!' he is the one showing me the benefits of what I'm doing and then bends over backwards to help out. He is very creative also, and when I'm stuck with thinking of marketing ideas, he is always coming up with new ways of getting my name out. He is one of my biggest marketers!"

Surviving the Transition

In this section we want to share with you the truth—the cold, hard facts—about the world you are about to enter. You are headed for a period we call *transition*. Since you are a mother, you probably have heard that word at least one other time in your life, and most of us know how that felt! Let's just say that *that* transition was a cakewalk compared to the transition you are about to experience.

A typical day will begin with you rising early, fixing breakfasts, and if necessary, dashing the older ones off to the bus stop, making beds, sorting laundry, and washing dishes. Sounds glamorous, doesn't it? Wait, there's more.

At some point you will plunk the little one down in front of *Barney* and make a start on your "to do" list. You may be interrupted several times, and the mere act of making the list will no doubt end up on your list.

On the list? The office-supply store, the local printer, the local newspaper to drop off an ad outline, and last but not least, the grocery store to pick up ingredients for the evening meal. It will all seem very well planned, very well thought out, and just as you have everyone bundled up and buckled in, the baby will have a messy diaper, and your two-year-old will throw up in the backseat all over your newly created ad outline.

Go ahead, cry. You'll feel better. Clean up the baby, wipe off your two-year-old, and tidy up the car and eventually, *if* you hit all the green lights, you will be home before the 11:00 P.M. news. If you think we're kidding, ask any mom with a business at home. She can tell you stories that will curl your hair!

The undertaking you are considering is not an easy task. You are sure to second-guess yourself on this very life altering decision more than once, and when you do, don't forget to take a step back and remember *why* you wanted to stay home. No matter how hard some days will seem, for you, staying home is the right move, and so it's on to tomorrow.

There are ways to cope with the transition pains you will no doubt experience, whether it's the longing for adult companionship or an identity crisis because you had been so wedded to your career. Networking will be your saving grace. You'll be amazed at how many other moms feel the same way. Find out everything you can about the local networking groups in your area—ask friends, neighbors, and other mothers at home if there are any groups in your area specifically targeted toward mothers in home-based business—then carefully select one or two organizations and get involved. You will learn more about networking and its tremendous value in Phase II of this book.

Like most of us, you will probably find the adjustment period difficult, but at some point you will realize that you have actually settled in to your routine quite nicely and learned to combine the adult world of business with the often chaotic world of caring for your children.

There are many things you can do to help yourself through the trying times—the days when you find yourself making breakfast in your high heels and business suit because your sole intention is to make a mad dash to the car, race to the office, and beg for your job back before your little ones lick the last traces of pancake syrup from their fingertips. Stick around, it's only going to get better. You will survive—here are a few tips.

■ *Set aside a period of time each day for you.* Resist the temptation to tidy up the house, work on your business, or fold laundry during your child's nap time and try to do something for yourself instead. Make sure you do something you enjoy. We equate this act to filling up the gas tank on your car. You replenish the tank, it keeps on going. You drive on relentlessly, it will eventually quit.

■ *Have lunch with friends or former colleagues regularly.* It's important for you to keep your connections and enjoy adult company once in a while. Arrange to leave the kids with a friend, a neighbor, or your husband and don't forget to plug your business; you never know where it can lead.

■ *Reward yourself.* When you reach a goal, make sure you pat yourself on the back; after all, you're the boss. Buy yourself a gift, write yourself a check, or treat someone special to dinner.

▪ *Exercise every day.* It will do wonders for your mind as well as keeping your body in check. Put the baby in a stroller and take a walk, visit the health club (make sure they have a nursery), or just jump on the stationary bike at home. Set aside just twenty minutes a day for exercise and you may be amazed at the fresh frame of mind and energy you get back!

▪ *Toot your own horn.* Celebrate your decision. Call friends, relatives, and those close to you and tell them all about your new business and your new role as a home-based entrepreneur. Keep your conversation positive and your excitement high.

▪ *Be creative and perhaps a little self-indulgent in your office setup.* Phase I of this book includes a very thorough section discussing how to pull your home office together. Make your office a special place you enjoy being in.

▪ *Invest in some basic equipment at the start.* Most of us rely heavily on our portable phones (to escape the sounds of noisy youngsters if necessary!), and a fax machine is worth its weight in gold.

Following these rules for surviving the transition, you will quickly come to love your new lifestyle and your new business. You may be surprised to find yourself feeling sorry for anyone stuck in a high-rise on a beautiful spring day as you take an afternoon walk with your child and enjoy the smell of new beginnings in the air.

Take a deep breath; your road trip to becoming a home-based business mom has just begun. It will be hard and fun and exciting and rewarding and exhausting all at once, and in the end, you may not be able to imagine yourself doing anything else.

2

Your Business Options

We all know that the first thing you need to start a successful business is a good idea—or is it? You may already have a business idea in mind, and if you do, you're one step ahead of the rest. But if you're scratching your head wondering what you can do, a license or franchise arrangement might be the answer. You'll have to weigh the pros and cons of each as you choose the path that's right for you.

Starting a Business From Scratch

When you bake a cake from scratch, you start with just the raw ingredients—no premixed, premeasured packages and no foolproof method. You take the key ingredients and mix them up until they come together as batter. If the cake rises, it's a success; if not, it's back to square one. A "scratch" business is the same. You start with an idea, mix in some organization, time management, marketing skills, and a little luck and you will form a client base. It can be a recipe for success.

But it is the riskiest option. When you start a business from scratch, you are on your own. Your survival in the business world depends solely on you and your persistence, organization, and know-how. There are no parent companies to call for advice, no proven track record, no support systems with 800 numbers to help ease you out of a trouble spot. The beauty of starting and maintaining a scratch business is that you can accept all the glory of its success when the time comes. You can maintain the business, expand it, and grow with it for as long as you choose, knowing you are the founder and at the heart of its success.

Your first step will be to decide what type of business is best for you.

Note: Many moms find that selecting a business that's geared toward the needs of families and/or children results in a "friendlier" business environment and is less stressful than servicing a corporate clientele. Your clients will be understanding if your toddler chooses to practice his tantrum-throwing skills while you are on the phone. Consider it.

Turn Your Hobby Into a Business

You are much more likely to succeed in your home-based business if you're doing something you really enjoy. Whether it's a rediscovered hobby you found little time for over the years as you made your way up the career ladder or a new pastime you've discovered since becoming a mom, think about using it as a way to make money from home.

Crafting, for example, is a multimillion-dollar industry, and there are numerous craft fairs held all around the country for marketing your products. Many successful crafts businesses were started at home; just make sure that you have a space set aside in your home for making your products and storing your inventory. As your children grow older, they will probably enjoy helping you in your business.

When Judy Schramm started her "scratch" business, Judy's Maternity Rental, she turned her lifelong hobby of designing and sewing into a source of income. Her new business not only allowed her to spend more time with her newborn, it also filled a niche in the maternity-wear market.

"During my pregnancy my husband and I were invited to several events that called for relatively formal attire. I went shopping for one or two suitable maternity outfits but found nothing within the price range I had set. Luckily, I had always enjoyed designing and sewing my own clothes, so finally I made myself something to wear. Interestingly enough, at one of the events we attended—a semiformal office party—there were six other women in varying stages of pregnancy, none of whom were dressed appropriately for the occasion!

"After my son was born, I realized that I did not want to return to my job as an international marketing manager for a software firm—a position that required a lot of overseas travel and regular ten-to-twelve hour workdays. Having made that decision, I started to think of alternative ways to work yet still be home. I felt that I had stumbled on an obvious business idea—providing formal maternity wear at a reasonable price. Given my expertise in sewing and my knowledge of marketing, I knew this was something I would be able to do. Since it was also a business I could operate comfortably from home, I knew I had found the answer to my work-mommy dilemma!

"I started sewing when the baby was three months old, built up an inventory of thirty or so garments, and rented my first outfit three or four months later. I set up a special area in my home for the business and arranged for my clients to come at preset appointment times to try on and select their clothing. It proved to be an ideal business that bridged my need to work with my need to be Mom."

Take Your Job Home

Many moms find that, with a few minor adaptations, they can start a home-based business just by taking their job home. Teachers can become home-based tutors; administrative assistants can offer secretarial or personal organization services; accountants and attorneys can hang out their own shingle.

Nancy Long recently completed her term as president of the Women's Bar Association of the District of Columbia—quite a feat for a part-time lawyer! Nancy enjoyed a successful career as a trial attorney with a law firm in Washington, D.C., before having her first child in 1990 at the age of twenty-nine. She had assumed she would simply return to work once the baby was born but instead found herself resenting the time and energy demands that her career as a litigator imposed. "My decision to stay home full-time with my daughter was a difficult one, considering all of the time, energy, effort, and money I had put into my legal career. But I don't regret the decision. After a short period at home, I realized that maintaining my legal skills was a must and not a luxury. I knew that I wanted to return to the legal profession, but being home to raise my daughter was my first priority."

Nancy decided to learn an area of law that she could practice from home and invested some time and money into continuing-legal-education seminars so that she could specialize in business law. She negotiated an arrangement with a local law office to use their facilities as needed in exchange for a percentage of her income. Since then, Nancy has steadily built up a solid client base, had a second child, and continues to run her practice from her home.

Try Something New

For some moms, motherhood brings with it a radical change of perspective and a transformed view of the world. These are the moms who will try something completely different from their former careers—often getting involved in baby, child, or mom-related products or services.

Mary Mitchell Peters made a drastic career change after she became a mom. Her fourteen-year career in telecommunication sales and marketing management gave way to founding the Maternity Network, Inc., a comprehensive resource for expectant and new parents. "Having a child completely and utterly changed every aspect of my life. I used to have no trouble working seventy hours a week, leaving little time for anything else in my life. When I had my son, I completely reprioritized. The business I chose to start perfectly combined my sales, marketing, and management skills with the firsthand experience of the maternity industry I had gained through my pregnancy. I'm now thirty-nine, pregnant with my

Home-Based Businesses That Work Well for Moms

Accounting
Architect
Association Management Service
Bill-Auditing Service
Bookkeeping
Book Sales
Business-Plan Writer
Calligraphy
Childbirth Coach
Child Care
Children's Theater Coordinator
Collection Agency
Computer Consultant
Computer Trainer
Computer-Maintenance Service
Copywriting
Cosmetic Sales
Courier Service
Crafts
Data Entry
Desktop Publishing
Direct-Mail Service
Doula Service
Dressmaking/Tailoring
Dried-Flower Arranging
Editor
Events Planning
Executive-Search Firm
Gift Services
Graphic Design/Art
Herb Farming
Image Consultant
Indexing Service
Interior Design/Decoration
Internet-Search Firm
Janitorial Service

Lactation Consultant
Landscaping Service
Mailing Service
Management Consultant
Marketing Consultant
Medical-Billing Service
Medical-Claims Processing
Medical-Transcription Service
Organizing Service
Party Clown/Storyteller/Entertainer
Party Planning
Payroll Service
Personal-Fitness Trainer
Personal Shopper
Pet Care (sitting, grooming, training)
Photographic Services (photo maintenance, albums)
Plant Service (maintenance, "sitting," delivery)
Public Relations
Publishing (newsletters, books)
Researcher
Resumé Service
Tax Preparation
Technical Writer
Telephone Sales/Marketing (only when the children are napping)
Toy Sales
Training (all types)
Tutoring
Vacation Planner
Wedding Planner
Word Processing
Writer
Yoga Teacher

second child, and I easily have the best balance I have ever had in my life between family, career, and outside activities."

The Recipe for Success

"The Recipe for Success" is simply a combination of what you are good at, what you enjoy, and what you know. And your business needs to meet all three criteria to be successful.

You know you have to like your new business; if you don't, you won't succeed. There is no one pushing you to get to a desk by 9:00 A.M.; there is no authority figure to answer to. You're it.

You know you have to be good at your business, because you'll have to set yourself apart from your competition and convince customers that you are the best provider of the particular product or service they need.

Last but certainly not least, you need to know what you're doing. Nothing turns customers off more than incompetence. The more you know, the better you will be.

The table below will help you get started by pinpointing your talents, skills, and personal preferences. Here's an example of how it works. Anna Mitchell was the manager of a furniture store before she had her daughter. She loved working with clients and using her flair for design to help them plan their home decor. But she wasn't sure how those skills and interests would translate into a home-based business. Anna filled out her table as follows:

What I Like	What I'm Good At	What I Know
(Working with people)	Design and decorating	(How to manage an office)
Design and decorating	(Sales)	Design and decorating
Shopping	(Working well with the public)	Furniture and textiles
Sewing	Organizing	Bookkeeping
(Managing)	(Cooking)	Marketing
(Sales)	Finding bargains	Pricing strategies
Antiquing	Entertaining	
Cooking		

After completing her table, it was immediately obvious to Anna that her talents, skills, and knowledge pointed to a business in the field of home design and decorating. Additionally, many of the other complementary skills she identified in the table, such as sales, managing, and working well with people would improve her chances for business success.

Grab some paper, make your own table, and take your time when filling in your categories. Circle anything that ends up in more than one category. Pay very close attention to those that end up in all three.

After completing your table, study it carefully and note the things that came to mind first; they are probably your best bet. You can build a business out of almost any interest—as long as it is something marketable. Ask yourself, "Would I be interested in obtaining this product or service?" and "Would I be willing to pay for it?" Get some feedback from friends and family members or put together a focus group or a survey.

Judy Harff started her business, A Bolder Image, even before she became pregnant with her first child! Knowing that she wanted to be home once she started a family, Judy had to find a way to do so and came to the conclusion that she should start her own business. Because she had no business experience, Judy began the process of investigating and researching the business possibilities, finally opting for desktop publishing, a field that was completely new to her but one she felt she had an aptitude for.

Judy invested in a computer system, took classes in desktop publishing design and software, and sought advice on running a business from a local women's mentoring program. By the time her first child arrived in 1995, Judy already had a head start on her business and had ironed out many of the "wrinkles" in her new enterprise. Obviously, Judy had to make some changes in her routine after giving birth, but she soon adjusted to working around the baby's schedule, and her business continued to grow.

Judy began her business as a relative novice, but through hard work, determination, and a commitment to the business, she has become extremely proficient at her craft. Although she admits that some of the more challenging projects initially filled her with trepidation, she soldiered on, mastering new skills over time. As a result, she is now able to offer a much wider range of services and can charge much more for her time. Her experience has also given her the confidence to nudge her business in a new direction and capitalize on the growing need for online multimedia design services.

Choosing to start a business in a completely new arena can be a gamble, but Judy's experience shows that with the right approach the payoff is worth the risk.

Buying a License or Franchise

Many moms know they want to start a business but either don't know how or see no sense in reinventing the wheel if they can purchase a license or franchise from an established, successful organization. If you know you want to run a business but you're not really interested in doing all the legwork required in starting from scratch, you might want to consider this option.

When you buy a license or franchise, you are buying a package deal, or "business in a box." Licenses and franchises differ greatly in what they offer, what they cost, and what state guidelines they must follow. They also differ significantly in success rates.

The Licensing Option

A very popular and often inexpensive way to get started is through licensing. If you think you don't know what licensing is, guess again. Have you ever been invited to a Tupperware party, Discovery Toys event, or Pampered Chef demo? Have you ever had a very enthusiastic individual with picture-perfect makeup offer to save your skin from the imminent signs of aging? If you answered yes, then you've had experience with licensed businesses—marketed too often, unfortunately, as "get rich quick" schemes.

The problem with most of these businesses is that they rely on your ability to recruit "downlines" of others whose success or failure is instrumental to your own success. Unfortunately, of the millions who sign up, only a few have the entrepreneurial spirit to keep going through countless rejections, no-shows, and cancellations. You must be prepared to be disappointed, discouraged, and dismayed at some point during your first few encounters as you attempt to build your empire.

Our suggestion? Take licensing for what it's worth. You probably won't earn very much money, but you might make more per hour than you would in other part-time opportunities. Do your homework—make sure the company is legitimate and the income potential it promises you is realistic—*before* you commit your time and money.

Let's say you are recruited by a multilevel skin-care company. You ask your best friend to book a party, you send out invitations, spend two hours doing the presentation, and sell $250 worth of products to your demo guests.

You, in turn, order the products and pay $165 (including handling charges) to the parent company or main distribution center, leaving you with a balance of $85. After all is said and done and all the products are delivered to your clients, you will probably have spent a total of five hours or so. Looking at it this way, your hourly income is $85 divided by your five hours of work—$17 per hour.

The upside of licensing is that it is generally a relatively inexpensive way to begin your business. You will usually receive a manual or two and perhaps a name badge or token pin. Be prepared to pay for all your presentation supplies, inventory, brochures, order forms, and other additional paraphernalia the parent company will want to sell to you.To be successful as a licensee, you will need to be aggressive and extremely persistent in your attempts to persuade your friends, family, and former colleagues to book parties, demonstrations, or better yet, sign up as distributors themselves.

You can find more detailed information on companies that offer licensing opportunities in business-opportunity magazines—generally available at your local bookstore. These periodicals appear regularly and will have the information you need to make a wise choice.

Here are some advantages to owning a license:

- Because a license is comparatively inexpensive, you don't have as much to lose if you find that the business you have chosen is not for you. Chalk up any financial loss to the cost of education. Regard each business experience as a stepping-stone to your ultimate goal of owning a business that is profitable and right for you.

- You will undoubtedly have a support system. Most licensing companies work on levels. The higher the level you reach, the more "new recruits" you will have working beneath you. Your recruiter will act in a mentoring capacity (as you will to your recruits), and she will be there to answer questions or help you solve problems.

- When you purchase a license, you are purchasing the rights to use a preexisting business plan. The entire business system has been well planned and well thought out; the target market, identified; and the product or service, perfected. There is little for you to do besides set up shop and begin operating.

- You can benefit from the licensor's reputation. As long as your community is not saturated with similar licensees, you will have a head start by offering a product or service that is already in demand.

- There are no royalties. Once you purchase a license, you will probably have no further financial obligation to the licensing company.

Here's the not-so-good news:

- Saturation. In a successful licensing system, the most money is made by those who get in earliest. By the time most of us learn about the latest and greatest way to make a fortune, drive a pink Cadillac, or retire early on, the market will have already reached a saturation point. Everyone you meet will have either bought, sold, or heard about the product, and therefore your new client base will be limited. It's tough to have a successful party if no one comes. Even if you do get in early, expect saturation at some point. Even those who have been with a product for years find it difficult to reach new clients. Innovation in your marketing is the key. We'll discuss how to be a successful marketer in Phase III.

- Another difficult part of the business of licensing is convincing people to trust and purchase your product. Also, the products are often fairly expensive, and it will be a challenge for you to sell them. You will need to establish strategies early on to develop a loyal customer following and ensure your "reorder" rate.

- You will need to keep inventory on hand which not only takes up space; you will be billed for it up front and will only realize a profit after you sell it all. Often it is only necessary for you to purchase a start-up kit—a sample of products for you to present to your potential clients. But your recruiter will try to persuade you to buy a larger amount so that you can offer your clients quick delivery from your stock. Our advice? Don't invest in a large number of products until you have made a few sales and are sure of your ability to sell and continue in this particular business.

- Hidden costs. Sales slips, brochures, order forms, postcards, samples, etc.—you will need them all, and you will pay for them all. You must have many "trade tools" on hand when setting up shop and conducting business. Most of these costs will be lumped in with your marketing expenses, since they will assist you in presenting your product to your public. Additional wardrobe for presentations may be necessary, and you will need to set aside funds for baby-sitters when you hold parties or presentations.

- No regulation of individual distributors. Although you may be operating your business within the parent company's recommended guidelines, someone else may not be, and that will reflect negatively on the entire company. We've all met that manic marketer who will not take no for an answer and sours us on that company's products forever afterward. Unfortunately, there is not much you can do about this, it may be the price you pay for buying a license rather than a franchise. If you want to be sure that *everyone* follows the rules, stay with a franchise system.

- No guarantees of territorial rights. Occasionally, someone might work her way up into a "regional position," but that position can be easily taken away if the sales in that area or within that division begin to fall.

- The sour-grapes syndrome. For former distributors who got in, sold little, enjoyed little, and got out, your business opportunity or licensing system is dirt to them. They will be the first to tell all those around how utterly awful and unsalable (never mind that they didn't market!) the product was, how high-pressure the regional managers were, and how boring and predictable the demonstrations were. They will be your worst enemy and one with which you will have to contend. You will discover your strengths in dealing with these individuals and will need to develop counterarguments to market successfully.

Often the best licensing opportunities are those that sell products you would be using and enjoying, anyway—toys, cosmetics, children's books, cooking equipment, and so on. If worse comes to worst and you decide the business isn't for you, at least whatever stock you have invested in will be put to good use!

The Franchise Option

A franchise is a regulated, organized business system that you purchase from a parent company or an individual operating as a company. By regulated, we mean that they are actually required by law to take certain steps to protect you, their consumer.

The Federal Trade Commission (FTC) sets the standards that must be adhered to, and a good franchising company will issue you a franchise offering circular (FOC) or disclosure document that is easy to read and understand and meets all FTC requirements.

Unfortunately, since the FTC is unable to police all franchise companies and their operating procedures, it simply assumes that each franchiser is in compliance. You should check with both your state's Better Business Bureau and attorney general's office for any complaints about the company you are considering.

Entrepreneur magazine lists the top-500 franchises and several more in their Annual Franchise 500 every January. Additionally, local franchise expos are frequently held around the country. Not all—in fact, a very small percentage—are designed to be run as home-based businesses.

When you contact a franchiser for information, you should receive detailed information about the franchise, the potential consumers, and what your start-up costs and recurring royalties would be. Be wary of those who seem vague or noncommittal. The FTC requires that no guaranteed-income claims are made and that all information pertinent to the daily operation of your business is disclosed.

Do not deal with any franchise company that charges you for its information packet or disclosure document and franchise agreement. Also, take the time to contact some of the franchisees listed in the company's disclosure document and find out how their business is doing and what kind of support they receive from the parent company. When you buy a franchise, you are buying the help and guidance the parent company offers you as part of the package. You pay for this service with "royalties"—a specified percentage of your gross receipts that you pay to the parent company. Royalties vary but on average range from 7 to 12 percent. Remember—the lower the royalty, the less support you should expect and the more self-sufficient you should plan to be.

Here's the good news about buying a franchise:

- Franchises are regulated by the FTC. They must follow specific rules that protect the franchisee. If you suspect you have not been treated properly, you may file a report with the FTC.

- When you purchase a franchise, you purchase the rights to a name as well as a system. If the name is one that is recognizable in your area, or nationally, you will have a head start in getting your business off the ground. Your arrival will be anticipated and warmly received.

- All the groundwork is done for you. Your job is to study and implement all of the policies, procedures, marketing tools, and guidelines that the franchiser has issued. Camera-ready logos and trademarks are supplied, saving you graphic-design expenses as well as trademark registration and research.

- The franchiser has already made (and hopefully corrected!) most of the missteps in setting up the franchise system before selling the system to you and other franchisees. You have the advantage of being told what to do and what *not to do* in order to run a successful franchise system.

- Support. You can pick up the phone, talk to an officer or agent of your parent company, and get help. When you start a scratch business, you are on your own; there is no support system for your business. Particularly in the early years, it is comforting to know that there is someone you can call when you run into a problem.

- Proven track record. If the parent company has many successful franchisees, clearly their operation is a success and their franchise system is a good one.

Here's the bad news about owning a franchise:

- You are bound to a system and must stick to all the rules and restrictions issued by the parent company. You may not in any way (whether you consider it a positive change or not!) alter the franchise system or service you offer. The franchise system relies on consistency throughout its operations, and you must maintain that consistency or face serious consequences, possibly even fines and legal fees. If you are naturally creative and prefer to work autonomously, such strictures may be frustrating.

- Royalties can be expensive. Some companies set their royalties very high and then set quotas for you. The more you earn, the more they earn; therefore, your success is necessary to their well-being. But you are operating the franchise, after all, and you may feel robbed if the franchiser takes more than a very small percentage of your gross receipts.

- The contract you sign is sure to be a term contract. This means that at some point your contract will come up for renewal for a nominal fee. You may never, depending on how a contract is set up, own your franchise for life. You will always need to be prepared to renew for a price.

- Don't assume that you are buying the rights to a territory or proscribed area of operation when you purchase a franchise. Look carefully at the disclosure document sent to you, as you may be able to negotiate some territorial protection.

- Franchise systems tend to be expensive. After all, you are purchasing a turnkey operation. If you subsequently discover that this particular type of business is not for you, there is no easy way out. You must be prepared to keep the business viable if you want to recoup any of your initial investment, and if you close for even a short period of time, you may find that you have relinquished your rights to that franchise.

- It is hard, although not impossible, to find a franchise that can be operated from home. Franchises, such as accounting and tax services, computer-related activities, mail order, and direct mail are examples of home-based franchise opportunities you could explore.

A final word about franchises: Often a franchise works because the system precedes it, and the name has a definite advantage. At other times, it is the nature of the product or service provided that makes a type of business work *whether it is a franchise or not*. Before you invest in this expensive business option, consider starting your own scratch business on a smaller scale.

The Online Connection

The Internet, the World Wide Web—whatever you call it, there's no doubt that increasing numbers of home-based business owners are finding ways to exploit this new powerful medium. Going online is a natural for individuals who work from home because it can connect you to the world outside in a couple of keystrokes.

Moms who work from home use their online connections in a number of different ways. Some run businesses they developed specifically to capitalize on the long reach and immediacy of the Internet. Others find their online service an invaluable link to the world beyond their doors, where they find support, respect, and validation from other moms who work from home. Still others use the Internet as a marketing tool—to reach millions of people relatively inexpensively in a way no other marketing tool can. And although many people aren't comfortable enough to actually *make* their purchases online, using a website to promote your business can provide prospects with enough information, including pictures, to make a buying decision and then follow up with a telephone call to place an order.

Amy Reis Levitt started her personalized-gift business, Amydoodles, three years ago so that she could be at home with her two children, now six and four years old. "My background is customer service–oriented, and I love to shop! So when I discovered that I could shop for my business and carry all sorts of great and unique things, I knew this was for me! I love to help people find gifts they need to get for themselves or others. I can help find gifts for birthdays, weddings, favors, baby gifts, corporate, Mother's and Father's Day, teacher gifts—anything someone needs."

Amy's business was given a big marketing boost when she expanded it to the Internet one year later. Her web page allows her to describe her range of products and personalization options more fully and less expensively than a four-color brochure would cost, and it is easy to update the site with special offers and promotions.

Other enterprising moms have actually built their businesses around this technological phenomenon. Phyllis Smith is an information professional with a master's degree in library and information sciences. Through her company, In the Know, Phyllis offers research services, which she fulfills by accessing commercial databases and a wide range of print and Internet resources. She is also developing a service to help other small-business owners launch websites that are "content rich and not simply online brochures."

Not suprisingly, Phyllis says that "online services are the tools of my trade. I couldn't function in this field without them. The Internet gives me access to fee-based systems that I might have to pay long-distance charges to access. It also gives me so many alternatives that I can avoid the fee-based systems to some degree."

Cheryl Demas, publisher of WAHM.com, an online newsletter for work-at-home moms, is another mom who has found a way to exploit the medium and make money from it. She says: "I wouldn't be in business without the Internet. I started my business designing websites, and I also started writing about my experiences searching for a home business. The first project was WebMoms—I wanted to help other moms work from home. I then expanded that and started WAHM.com. With it I'm able to provide tips, advice, opportunities, etc., for many different types of businesses. The mailing list is also a great source of support for many women and the site is getting over 100,000 page hits per month. Now I'm so busy with WAHM.com that I'm not doing the Web-design work anymore."

Other moms find the online support invaluable and use news groups and mailing lists for support and networking. Take Nancy Johnson, for example: Nancy is a consultant with Discovery Toys, a multilevel marketing organization that comes with a built-in support system of other consultants and managers. Still, Nancy finds going online helpful: "Discovery Toys has a message board, or bulletin board, that is very helpful to network with other consultants and share ideas. My up-line has an E-mail loop to keep us informed and pass on inspiration. I have also met other moms online who have requested catalogs and career information."

If you're looking for advice, resources, suppliers and wholesalers, or reference information on virtually anything, the Internet's powerful search engines make it easy to locate exactly what you need to know.

If you decide you need to be online, too, shop around carefully for the best deal. You'll also need a modem (28,800 baud rate or higher is best) to dial out. Once you're "connected," you'll wonder how you ever lived without it!

Protecting Yourself From Work-at-Home Scams

We've all seen the ads and their seductive promises: "Would you like to work at home? Many people are earning hundreds of dollars in their spare time."

Sounds too good to be true? That's because it is. Most of these ads get your interest by telling you how much money you can make, how easy it is, and how quickly you can become rich. Work-at-home ads range from a few lines in the classifieds to full-page "testimonials" in magazines. So-called opportunities range from stuffing envelopes to becoming a "disability consultant" and earning "$5,000 plus, monthly."

The organizations behind these schemes know how many people are desperately looking for a way to make money from home—and they exploit that need. Many of them end up being investigated for fraud by the FTC. The most common schemes include:

Envelope Stuffing

Although it's menial, boring work, envelope stuffing sounds like a relatively easy way to earn extra money, especially for moms who already have a lot on their plate. The ads generally ask you to send a small fee for information. Unfortunately, all you will most likely receive in return is a letter instructing you to place the same ad you responded to in your local newspapers and magazines or to send it to friends and relatives. You will only make money by doing the same thing as the original advertiser—at the expense of others.

Craft Assembly or Home Sewing

Ads that promise really good money for assembling products and crafts or making simple things like baby bibs and aprons should immediately spark your fraud antennae! They will require you to invest hundreds of dollars of your own money in equipment and supplies, and then they will usually reject your finished products because they failed to meet "quality standards."

Chain Letters

These nasty things have been around forever, but now some unscrupulous individuals are using them to make money. These days, they take various forms, but all of them ask you to send money to a number of people listed in the letter and then make copies and send it to a number of your own friends. Basically, it's a pyramid scheme, and illegal. Chain letters should be turned over to your local postmaster so that the initiators can be found and prosecuted.

Internet Schemes

The Internet is a wonderful resource for home-based entrepreneurs, but it can be dicey if you're hoping to find a business opportunity there. If you are online already, you have no doubt received tons of unsolicited E-mail offers to "make your fortune from home." For scam artists the Internet is the ultimate fantasy—a way of reaching thousands of people at an extremely low cost. But we haven't yet found any Internet offer worth pursuing.

How Can You Tell What's Legitimate?

First, most legitimate operations won't ask for money from you unless you have already received information from them that clearly states what you will receive in return. Also, a legitimate organization will display not only their mailing address but their telephone/fax numbers, too. And when you call, they will be prepared to answer your questions (without charging you). Make sure you ask:

- What exactly will I have to do?
- How will I be paid, how often, and by whom?
- How much will my total up-front investment be? (Ask for an itemized list of expenses that includes supplies and raw materials; any fees; other expenses you will be charged before you can get started.)

You want to get all this information *in writing*. Then, if fraud is involved, you will have ammunition to take to either your local Better Business Bureau, the local postmaster, and/or the area's consumer-protection office.

The bottom line? It would be lovely to believe that making money from home was as easy as sending $19.95 to an address in the paper and then sitting back while your profits mounted. But remember, if it were really that easy to make that kind of money from home, wouldn't we all be doing it already?

3

Your Business Identity

If you decide to start your business from scratch, one of the first significant decisions you'll need to make is what to call your business. Don't skimp on this step. You're going to live with the name you choose for a long time!

You will no doubt agonize over the name, the spelling of it, its design, and possibly a logo that sums up your business identity graphically. If you don't agonize over these matters, you should. The name you choose for your business is the beginning of its identity.

What's in a Name?

Make sure that you choose a name that is memorable and easy to associate with your business activities. For example, Pam Smith decides to open her own catering company and chooses Smith and Co. as the name of her business. The name gives no indication of the type of business she is running or of the product or service she will provide. But if Pam instead names her business Smith's Creative Catering or Pam's Party-Planning Services, there will be no question about what her company does.

Choose a name that appropriately reflects the business image you want to project. If our friend Pam Smith were to start an executive-secretary business aimed at corporate executives, "Pam's Typing Services" would not impress the type of clientele she wants to attract. "Smith Executive Services," for example, has a much more "corporate" ring to it and immediately projects a more sophisticated image.

Your business name should be easy to say, easy to read, and most importantly, spelled conventionally. If not, you will spend much of your time spelling the name out to people or trying to cash checks that the bank won't accept because the payee doesn't match your business name!

Before you firmly decide on a name, you will want to make sure that it is not already in use locally or nationally registered and protected by the U.S. Patent and Trademark office.

Teri Runco learned the hard way about trademarks and trade names. After Teri had her fourth child, she invented a nursing blanket that would allow her to breast-feed her baby discreetly in public. Soon she was besieged by requests from other nursing moms who saw her using the product. Deciding to start a home-based business to manufacture and sell the blankets, Teri founded Peek-A-Boo Nursing Blankets.

Unfortunately, the day after she had picked up (and paid several hundred dollars for) her stationery order from the printer, the attorney she had retained to help her register her new business called to tell her that she could not use the name Peek-A-Boo. Mattel, the toy manufacturer, already owned it.

Needless to say, Teri regretted not taking the time to search before she started using the name. Happily, she has since obtained a patent for her invention, renamed her company Priv-A-See, and is currently waiting for the trademarking process to be completed.

Choosing a Logo

A logo is simply the way your business name is displayed visually. It can be basic—for example, how your name is written or spelled.

How to Conduct a Preliminary Trademark Search

As intimidating as it sounds, it's really quite easy (and often free!) to conduct a preliminary search to make sure that the name you want to use is available and unregistered.

Plan on spending some time at your local public library or online, if you have access. Either way, you should be able to access a national database provided by the U.S. Patent Trademark Library. Give your librarian the name or names you would like to have researched and she will be able to research previously registered trade names and trademarks on a state and federal level. Many counties offer you a maximum number of free online services or a maximum dollar amount each month. After you have exceeded the maximum, they may start charging you a nominal fee per request.

This is a great way to save yourself time, money, and frustation. You can make sure you are not infringing on anyone else's trademark, and by registering with the U.S. Patent Trademark Office, you are ensuring that you will never be forced to change your name.

More elaborate logos will generally include a graphic image or a symbol that is somehow tied to it. Your logo should appear consistently on all your printed materials—letterhead, business cards, advertisements, signs, etc. This is how you can begin to build a business identity that your customers will recognize and associate with you. For example, picture McDonald's without the golden arches or Toys 'R Us without the smiling giraffe or the reversed R. These and a host of other logos are part of our daily landscape. Without thinking, we associate them with the companies they represent. The most effective logos elicit the most automatic responses.

Since your logo will often be the first point of contact between you and your future clients, you will want it to start working for you

Sample Logos

Supercooks Inc.

TODDLIN' TIME ®
... A Whole New Way To Play

Kerry Landscapes

BITS 'N BYTES
YOUR COMPUTER SPECIALISTS

jellybeanz
handmade clothes for kids

The **Yoga Connection**

right away. Color, form, and font are all important in determining the look of your logo. It should also be market-appropriate. For example, if you are opening a home-based preschool, your logo should be bright, attractive, and playful. On the other hand, a sophisticated, abstract logo would be more geared toward the executive suite.

Don't rush the process. You don't want to end up with something you aren't thrilled with, because once you have committed it to print, it can be costly to start over.

When planning your business logo:

Do a little research on what you find effective. Pick up the newspaper, glance around, and let your eyes take you where they want to go. Pay close attention to where they stop. Is it an ad? Is it the name? The way it is written? An accompanying picture or design? Ask yourself what it is that made you stop, pay attention, and read that particular ad. Clip the ad for future reference.

Consult a professional. You don't have to be an artist to have an idea and sketch out some basic concepts, but we highly recommend that you contract a professional graphic artist or designer to execute your finished logo. Ask your local chamber of commerce or home-based networking group for a list of graphic artists in your area. Start noticing logos, and if you come across one that you find appealing, ask the business owner for a referral to the designer.

A good graphic designer will meet with you to discuss ideas and concepts and then present several variations for your review. Show her the ads you have clipped and tell her why you liked them. Ask for a project estimate at your first meeting that details what you will be billed for. Also, make sure that you will be informed when her charges have reached a predetermined cap. Don't be afraid to complain if you are not pleased with the finished product. After all, *you* are paying, and you should be satisfied with the outcome.

Choose a design, or a symbol that conjures up an appropriate image of your company to its target market. If the product or service you offer is fun in nature (e.g., entertainment for children's parties), your logo and any symbols associated with it should suggest that. If your business serves corporations (e.g., a human-resources consultant for large companies), your logo will need to be more conservative to be taken seriously.

If you are not sure how to define your business image, try this exercise. Imagine that you have been asked to write your name in a way that will help someone who has never met you learn about you. You want the way in which you write your name to reflect your individual personality, your strengths, your finer points. Now try it with your business name.

Choose a logo that will not lose visual quality when reduced or enlarged to fit various situations. A good logo should be easy to read in any size. The last thing you want is for your logo to appear in small print and be unrecognizable, even to you. For this reason, the simpler designs are usually better.

Avoid using clip art (available in software and in print) for your logo. Since the design is not unique, you will be unable to trademark it. On that same note, don't attempt to copy another company's logo. When it comes to company names or logos, imitation is most definitely *not* the sincerest form of flattery. Actually, it's the fastest way to a lawsuit!

Use color. Although it will add to the cost, even a small splash of color can add visual emphasis to a logo. Talk to your local printer; you may be pleasantly surprised to find that using two colors isn't that much more expensive than using only one. Your graphic artist will also have some insight and tips on color.

Once you have a finished logo, have several copies made in various sizes. You will need crisp, clean copies of what advertisers call *camera-ready art* for every ad you run.

Consider trademarking. We aren't suggesting that you run out and spend over two hundred dollars to register your name and design before your first client walks through the door, but you don't want to wait too long, either. You are going to invest time, effort, and energy into establishing a business with a unique identity. You don't want to be forced to change your name simply because someone else trademarked it first.

4

Setting Up Shop

It is no accident that large companies spend hundreds of thousands of dollars in order to create an inviting office environment. Many of us have worked in office buildings that have beautiful lobbies with live plants and comfortable chairs; soft, inviting color schemes; and full-service cafeterias. All these things combined create a pleasant place to work, which after all, will often mean pleasant, happy employees who do just that—work.

You have already chosen to trade in that beautiful atmosphere for one a little less glamorous. Sneakers and sweats will replace the fancy wardrobe, your kitchen (complete with mess!) will replace the coffee shop, and instead of stepping off the elevator onto plush carpet, you will undoubtedly stumble downstairs in the morning and step on a pile of Legos. With that kind of wake-up call, who needs caffeine! All in all, you'll need to make some adjustments—not impossible if you follow our suggestions for creating a comfortable, convenient workplace right in your home.

Choosing the Most Efficient Work Space

Your first and most important decision is *where* to set up shop. The size of the space you need will probably depend, in part, on the type of business you run. You may need only a small area that can accommodate a desk, phone, and filing cabinet. But if you need to store inventory, set up office equipment or machinery, and still have room for the essentials, you will need to make more room. If you do need a lot of storage space, it may make sense to consider having two separate areas—one that is readily accessible for doing paperwork and conducting day-to-day tasks and another area in a different part of the house that you can use for storage.

Now, before you hire the contractor to rearrange your walls or add another floor, understand that spare bedrooms, basements, alcoves, and even closets have all been converted into makeshift offices for home-based entrepreneurs! The key word is *innovation*— a word that is quickly becoming a part of your everyday vocabulary as a business builder!

Here are some guidelines for choosing the best possible work space for your business:

- Don't set yourself up at the dining room or kitchen table unless it is absolutely the last resort. These everyday areas are used for the family meal, doing homework, entertaining, and other family activities. Each time it is used for something other than your business, you will find yourself grudgingly clearing away your business papers. You will then face the time-consuming task of getting everything back where it was before you can get started again. Even the most organized of us will eventually wilt under these conditions.

- Choose an area that is convenient and easily accessible to the kitchen, bathroom, and children's play area.

- If possible, make sure your office space has a door you can close at the end of your day. Admittedly, one of the best things about working from home is being able to do the laundry and make dinner while simultaneously working on a business project. But, you need to be able to "leave work" at the end of your day, just as you did when you worked outside the home.

- Choose an area that is well lit, preferably with a window. No one wants to work in a dark, unwelcome area. If you don't enjoy being in your office, you will find excuses not to be there.

- Make sure the space you choose has adequate electrical outlets to handle your office equipment, especially if you will be using a computer, fax, multiline phone, etc. Consider hiring an electrician to install a few more outlets. If adding outlets is not an option, consider power strips. Just be careful not to overload your circuits.

- If the best option is your unfinished basement, consider stretching the budget to finish off at least a portion of it. You may be pleasantly surprised at how little it costs to finish off a small area and throw some carpet down. Make sure that any windows end up in your office and check that there is adequate heat. A cold, drafty office is not an inviting place to work.

- If possible, have an area close by where the children can play. A makeshift playroom isn't difficult to pull together no matter where your office is. A few toys, some coloring materials, and perhaps a TV and VCR will occupy little ones while you concentrate on your business, and you'll be able to keep half an eye on them while you catch up on your work.

- Once you have decided where your office will be, throw on a fresh coat of paint and add some personality. Favorite art (if you don't currently own much, consult your nearest toddler for some finger-painting masterpieces; he will be only too glad to assist), pictures of family (lots of the kids; after all, they are your incentive behind the whole project), and some attractive plants, will all help to make your space a personal and fun place to be.

- Make a sign for your office door. Have your husband or a friend take a photo of you sitting at the computer with a phone to your ear, and let your children know that when this is hanging on the door, Mommy is working and needs quiet—more wishful thinking than anything else when they are really young, but it's never too early to start teaching them this rule.

"Rotating" Toys

If your children are like ours, they probably lose interest in toys they have been playing with for a while. We've found that rotating toys is a successful way to keep a fairly constant supply of "new" ones available without making constant trips to the toy store. Take a bunch of toys and put them away somewhere. Every few months or so bring them out again and put away the toys they have lost interest in. You'll save money, the kids will stay happily occupied as they rediscover their toys, and you'll have more time to work!

■ Make sure that all family members understand the ground rules—that your office is your work space and is off-limits to them unless they have your permission to enter. We know from bitter experience that it is no fun entering your office ready to work, only to lose a half hour reorganizing and cleaning grape jelly off the keyboard!

■ If you intend to take a home-office deduction, the allotted space *must be dedicated exclusively to the running and operating of your business.* If *any* part of your office is seen to be used as a general family area or a play space for the kids, your deduction can be disqualified. Check with your CPA to get information on full compliance with IRS regulations.

By using these fairly simple guidelines, you should be able to transform some part of your home into an efficient, bright, and economical office. Sure, others get the fancy lobbies and the key to the executive bathrooms, but can they report to work in fuzzy slippers and a bathrobe? You will be the envy of all your former coworkers!

Who's Watching the Kids?

When Amanda started her desktop publishing business, she paid great attention to detail. She chose a good name and logo, put together an attractive marketing package, and hurried out to find clients. After only two meetings, she acquired a rather large account that promised to get her business off to a healthy start. Amanda worked far into the night to finish projects for her new client and often early in the morning before her six-month-old and three-year-old sons awoke. Some nights, thanks to earaches, teething troubles, or restless children, Amanda got little or no sleep at all. Amanda abandoned her business after only a few months. She was simply too tired to carry her workload and take care of two children at the same time.

Six months later, Amanda ran into her friend Vicky, who also worked at home managing a desktop publishing service and was doing quite well. When Amanda asked, incredulously, how Vicky was managing to juggle everything, Vicky replied that she dropped her two children off with a neighbor three mornings a week. The kids welcomed the change of scenery and enjoyed being with other children, her neighbor appreciated the extra income, and Vicky was comfortable knowing that her little ones were just two doors down and would be back with her in time for lunch. After hearing of Vicky's success, Amanda wondered if perhaps, with a little more planning, there couldn't have been a better outcome for her business.

Unfortunately, there are many like Amanda who begin their business with lots of enthusiasm and grand plans, only to find there is just no time to implement them. We have found that one of the most likely reasons for a mom to give up her business in frustration is the difficulty handling and juggling all her responsibilities. Days are filled with kids, household chores, meal preparation, and laundry, followed by evenings, nights, and early mornings spent on the business. This can exhaust even the most energetic supermom.

You may be thinking, Wait! I thought I was working at home to *avoid* child care! True. But you can't expect to run a business without a reliable block of time each day or at least each week, when the children aren't underfoot. You don't have to find full-time day care for your children. Just be innovative about finding time to work. Consider the following:

- *Get creative with barter.* Find friends, neighbors, or relatives who will take your kids for a few hours in exchange for either a few child-free hours themselves or a discount or preferential rate on the product or service your business offers.

- *Hire a mother's helper.* We haven't met an adolescent yet who wasn't thrilled with the opportunity to earn a little extra pocket money. For just a few dollars an hour, you can hire a responsible teen or preteen to come to your home and keep your little ones happily occupied while you work. Scheduling help from 3:00 P.M. to 6:00 P.M. several days a week will boost your quality work time considerably.

Choose a mother's helper who seems responsible and enjoys children. He or she should be energetic and ready to entertain your child. Anything less and your afternoon will probably be punctuated by constant interruptions as your children come looking for Mommy. Stay in control of their activities by having a game plan for your mother's helper to follow. If it's a nice day, suggest that she take the kids to a neighborhood park or playground or for a walk around the block. Keep a stack of fun arts and crafts projects for them to work on if the weather is bad.

Finally, bear in mind that if you have one or more infants, you'll want to look for an older teen who has some experience with babies.

- *Check out local child-care drop-in programs.* These are great if all you need is a couple of mornings a week to call on prospects, attend meetings, or have some uninterrupted work time. Most communities offer such programs one, two, or three mornings a week.

- *Consider a cooperative preschool.* Cooperatives fill the niche nicely for moms who want some real involvement in their children's child care and are generally less expensive than other options. But you will be expected to contribute a certain amount of time each month, which may become a burden as your business grows.

- *Look into part-time day care in someone's home.* This option works well because it usually benefits both parties. Often a mom who has chosen to stay home and start her own in-home day-care business will be much more flexible than a commercial day-care center. By arranging to drop your child or children off two or three

Child-Care Ground Rules

If you haven't left your child in a day-care setting before, you may feel a little uneasy at first. Following some basic ground rules will not only set your mind at rest; it will also help ensure a good relationship with your child-care provider.

- Check for a clean, safe environment and don't hesitate to ask for references.
- Agree on a set number of hours that you will bring your child each week and then drop off and pick up your child promptly each time. Give your provider plenty of notice if you need to change the arrangement for any reason, add or reduce hours, plan vacation time, and so on.
- Never take your child if she is sick or running a fever unless you have okayed it with your provider first.
- Leave a list of telephone numbers you can be reached at, plus cell phone and pager number, if necessary.
- Fill out an emergency medical authorization in case your child has an accident and needs immediate medical attention. Make a photocopy of your child's medical ID card and attach it to your signed form.
- Respect your child-care provider as you would any other business owner. Her cooperation and support will help your business grow.

mornings or afternoons a week, you can buy yourself a chunk of time at a reasonable price and help support your day-care provider's home-based business as well. If you find the right person and setting for the job, it can definitely be a win-win situation.

- *Take advantage of family.* If you are lucky enough to have a parent or other relative nearby, make the most of it! Encourage Daddy to plan a special weekend outing with the kids once or twice a month and use the time to get caught up on paperwork or other non-urgent projects you haven't been able to get to.

A Personal Glimpse Gloria Ecks actually built her business around the day-care needs of moms so that *she* could stay home with her own children.

Gloria didn't want to go back to her teaching job after her first child was born, but she did want to earn some income to replace her former earnings. As it happened, a neighbor who needed before- and after-school child care for her children asked Gloria if she wanted to provide it. Gloria agreed, and as word spread in the neighborhood, she soon found herself responding to requests for full-time day care for some of the younger children, too. Before long, Gloria and husband Doug had converted their basement to accommodate Gloria's Kidcare, filling the space with toys, child-size tables, and age-appropriate learning games and apparatus.

It seemed a natural progression to add a more structured preschool a few years later, when Gloria's "backyard" neighbor, Joan (who had just given up teaching following the birth of her third child), agreed to help her run a preschool for two-year-olds. Together they developed a curriculum and began to operate G & J's Playschool from Gloria's basement one morning a week.

But as the preschoolers grew, so did Gloria's business! The following year she and Joan began a preschool for three-year-olds to accommodate their graduates. At the same time, many of the day care kids were turning two, and the preschool for two-year-olds quickly filled as well! Both programs were thriving, so eventually Gloria cut back on her day-care service so she could concentrate on the preschool and part-time toddler programs, and still have time to volunteer at her children's school several afternoons each week.

Nine years later, Gloria feels no desire to return to the school system. She knows she is offering a valuable service and enjoys "watching the little ones learn and grow." She runs her business professionally: parents are given written instructions on drop-off and pickup times, payment terms, and holidays (she follows her local school district's calendar), and Gloria gets to take a well-deserved break during school vacations. She is doing something she enjoys, earning the income she needs, and is home for her children. It's a solution that works for her.

Choosing Your Electronic "Staff"

One very nice part about being happily home based is that your support "staff" are always even-tempered, show up on time every day, and don't require a paycheck. The one drawback? You can't have a meaningful conversation with them, and don't expect them to treat you to lunch. They're machines.

Computers, fax machines, personal copiers, answering systems, calculators, and a host of other useful and often fun little items will together work well for you and help pull your daily workload. Sometimes it's the most unassuming little gadget that you find you cannot live without!

Personal Computers

As office-supply and electronics superstores have popped up all over the place, competition between the different chains has brought down prices and increased selection—all to our benefit as consumers. Today's standard personal computer setup offers more computing power, speed, reliability, and efficiency *less expensively* than a standard mainframe did as recently as ten years ago. This gives you a pretty good understanding of the awesome technological power available to a SOHO (small office/home office) business owner today.

What this means is that many start-up home-based moms will already have access to a pretty good computer system or can include one in their start-up budget. Check out the circulars that come with most Sunday papers for purchasing incentives, such as free software, free printers, expanded drives, etc. During the grand opening of one local super store, Tanya saved over a thousand dollars when she purchased a new system equipped with a free printer, free software, free mouse, CD-ROM, modem, and extended warranty—all for the same price she would normally have paid for just the hard-drive and monitor. It is definitely wise to shop around.

Here's our recommended list of electronic basics and what to look for in each:

Hardware   Computer technology is developing so quickly nowadays, the only thing you can be certain of is that your new state-of-the-art computer will be outdated practically as soon as you get it home! But the good news is, you won't need that newest cutting-edge model unless your business is in high-end computing applications.

The basics of your computer system are a monitor, a hard drive (to store the data), a processor (the engine of your system), and a printer. The gadgets commonly available now include a CD-ROM, fax/modem board, Zip drive for backup, and additional storage. But there is also a wealth of specialized tools available—color printers, laser printers, scanners, and other add-ons. If your business revolves around your computer, you know what you need. If not, go with a basic system, but make sure it is upgradable so that you can add to it as the need arises.

Software   Most computers come preloaded with a variety of commercial software—some of it useful but most of it "filler" to make you think you are getting a great deal! You will need at a minimum:

- A word-processing package for writing letters, reports, mailings, etc. (e.g., Word, WordPerfect);
- A database program to keep track of customer names and addresses, mailing lists, etc. (e.g., Access, Paradox);
- A desktop publishing program if you want to create your own brochures, fliers, and other graphic pieces (e.g., Publisher, PageMaker);
- A financial tracking or bookkeeping program to keep track of your income and expenses in the most efficient way (e.g., Quicken, QuickBooks);

- Online software. If you plan on marketing your business via the Internet, you will need software to let you access it (e.g., Netscape, Compuserve, America On Line, etc.).

Remember, if you are planning on writing off a computer as a business expense, it must be used solely for the business, not by other family members for school, entertainment, or other reasons.

Stand-Alone Fax

If you know you are going to be faxing a lot, it's worth investing in a stand-alone unit. If not, you may be able to make do with the fax/modem board that came with your computer. Remember, though, that everything you send will have to be entered into the computer first. Moreover, if your computer is down for any reason, your fax will be, too.

Your fax machine will be a huge time-saver. Instead of driving to the local newspaper to proof your ad or schedule a meeting with a client to discuss a document, you will be able to review and approve transactions from the comfort of your office. You will make orders, take orders, review drafts and contracts, and even place your lunch order—all by fax! Once again, shop around. Fax machines have come down in price over the past several years; you should be able to find a decent one for less than three hundred dollars. If you can afford to spend a little more, go with a plain-paper fax, because it will double as a low-volume copier.

All-in-One Machines

There is a trend to combine as many functions as possible in one piece of hardware that will sit on your desk, replacing maybe three or four machines, and cost less than buying each machine separately. It sounds attractive, especially if space is limited, but there are drawbacks: for one thing, if the machine breaks down, you will lose all those functions. Bottom line—if you are on a tight budget but really need a printer-scanner-copier-fax-answering machine and can't afford to buy all of the above, it might be a good short-term choice.

Copier

If you plan to publish manuals, distribute thick documents, or cut and paste ad copy, a copier may be worth the investment for you— as a time-saver alone. Remember, though, that they are expensive to maintain, and you may be able to save much more by planning a weekly trip to the local copy shop. If you do decide to purchase a copier, you'll find a wide range of prices and functionality. Shop around and consider buying a used machine if you can find one.

Answering Machine or Voice Mail

Although a recorded message is less appealing than a live voice on the receiving end of a call, there are times when you simply can't or don't want to take a phone call from a potential client. Answering machines or voice-mail systems can handle these calls for you at those times— professionally and cleanly. Just keep some basics in mind:

- Steer clear of machines that play annoying tunes or utilize impersonal computer voices. Also avoid machines that operate on computer chips, because they will lose all current incoming and outgoing messages if you experience a power outage or if your machine is accidentally unplugged.

- Do not have your children record the outgoing message if you expect to receive business calls on the line. It's generally pretty annoying on personal lines (we all think our kids are just the cutest thing, but...). For business calls, it's plain inappropriate and extremely unprofessional.

- Consider renting a voice mailbox through your local telephone company. This has the advantage of giving you a quasi–second line. That is, if you are on your line and another caller tries to get through, they will be diverted to your voice mail instead of getting a busy

Do You Need a Second Telephone Line?

The short answer is no, you don't *need* one. But installing a second line into your home will prove to be a worthwhile investment. And if you will be using a fax regularly or hooking up to an online service via modem, a second line will be a must. Locate the phone in your office and instruct the children to ignore that phone when it rings. Make sure it is hooked up to an answering machine or diverts incoming calls to voice mail when you are unable to answer it.

At first glance, a dedicated business line may seem to be an added expense you can do without, but your business line will become the secretary you don't have! It will receive calls when you are dealing with a crabby child or a house filled with kids over for a day of play. It will enable you to ignore the business phone on weekends— time that you might want to reserve for your family—and the separate bill you will receive from the telephone company will make your accounting much easier. All in all, the professionalism and convenience will be worth the initial expense.

Don't be surprised to discover that a business line costs more than a residential line. However, from a marketing standpoint, a listing in the business section of the telephone directory may make the additional expense worthwhile.

Call your local phone company to find out what special features they offer businesses. Conference calling, call forwarding, and voice mail are just a few of the available services you can obtain for a nominal fee.

signal or listening to your phone ring endlessly. Although in the long run it is more expensive to rent a voice mailbox than it is to purchase an answering machine, it is reliable, convenient, and can be expanded to offer more options as your business grows. Contact your local phone company for information about voice mail and its availability in your area.

■ Avoid using the service known as "call waiting" on your business line. It is very unprofessional to excuse yourself in the middle of a call to respond to the annoying little beep that signals another incoming call. Better to consider the voice-mailbox alternative mentioned earlier or get a second line that is tripped when the first line is busy.

Here are a few other things you shouldn't be without:

Portable Phone   This is definitely at the top of our list of gadget essentials. Murphy's home-based mom's law says that the minute you answer your business line because the kids are quiet is the precise moment that little voices reach a screaming pitch! This leaves you frantically grabbing your portable phone and making a beeline for the nearest closet with a door!

It's worth spending a little more to get a portable with the longest range possible, and the best sound quality. (Caroline was mortified to discover that her first, relatively inexpensive portable phone actually *amplified* the background noise of her three toddlers!)

Baby Monitor   If you don't have one, get one, especially if your office is going to be located on a different floor of the house. You can switch it on while the baby is napping and have the comfort of knowing that you will hear him if he stirs. (When Caroline had her fifth child, instead of buying a "baby monitor," she installed intercoms on various levels of the house, including the baby's room. The units cost less than the baby variety and are still useful today to communicate with kids who manage to wander into different areas of the house just when it's time for dinner!)

Clock   Don't waste time leaving your office to check the time; make sure it is convenient to your desk so that you don't need to turn full circle to check the time.

Calculator   No matter how good you are at math, you will need a calculator. Don't depend on the little pocket size. Purchase a desktop model that is either AC- or battery-powered. Although convenient, the solar-powered models are often inefficient in low light.

5

Financing Options

By now the wheels should be turning. You probably have a good idea of the type of business you plan to start, a name, possibly a logo, and the basic components for setting up your home office. Now, who's going to pay for all this?

If you need to start your office from scratch and finance the purchase of a computer, fax, and incoming phone lines or if you need to do some minor build-out to accommodate your office or to store inventory or working supplies, then your initial start-up costs may seem a little scary. Don't be intimidated; you have choices.

How Much Money Do You Need?

Your first step is to fill out our checklist on the following pages. By putting a check mark and an approximate cost in the spaces provided, you should be able to estimate how much you will need. We have left some blank spaces for you to add items if your business will need specialized equipment. For example, a caterer will need cookware and recipe books, a seamstress may need to invest in a more efficient sewing machine, and a salesperson may need product samples. Fill in these spaces as they apply to your business. Be thorough and don't be afraid to recycle. If you already have a good supply of paper, pens, and pencils around the house, use them! If you have an extra stapler, a bookshelf that's not being used, or an old bulletin board that's gathering dust, use them! Don't spend money for the sake of spending money. The less you spend to set up, the sooner you will be in the black and can start earning a paycheck.

After you complete the checklist, add five hundred dollars for a margin of error. You may be pleasantly surprised that when all is said, done, and paid for, you come in under budget. If so, keep the remainder in your business account as a small pillow to rely on for unforeseen future expenses.

Your Home Office Shopping List

Take this list with you to your local office-supply store(s) and price the items you know you will need. For your marketing supplies (business cards, letterhead, envelopes, etc.), contact your local printer for estimates. Check off each item or expense as you go.

Office Supplies		*Office Machines*	
Calendar	$	Computer	$
Address book	$	Fax machine	$
Receipt book	$	Copier	$
Paper	$	Answering machine	$
Pens and pencils	$	Baby monitor	$
File crates and folders	$	Portable phone	$
Stapler	$	Cellular phone	$
Postal scale	$	Pager	$
Manila envelopes	$	Software	$
Card-file box	$	Calculator	$
Return-address labels	$		
Return-address stamps	$		
Bank-account checks	$		
Accounting ledger	$		
Message pads or book	$		
SUBTOTAL	$_____		

Marketing

Logo design	$
Stationery	$
Business cards	$
Paper, at least two reams	$
Brochures	$
Presentation folders	$
SUBTOTAL	$_____

Professional Services

Accounting consultation	$
Legal consultation	$
Liability and business property insurance	$
SUBTOTAL	$_____

Licenses/Fees/Other Expenses

Phone hookup	$
Voice mail	$
Business license	$
Online service charge	$
Renovation/construction	$
SUBTOTAL	$_____

Specialized Equipment and Supplies

_____ $	
_____ $	
_____ $	
_____ $	
SUBTOTAL	$_____
TOTAL	$_____
add	$500
FINAL TOTAL	$_____

Add the subtotals together and then add five hundred dollars, the error margin mentioned earlier. This figure should adequately cover the expenses of setting up your office. Obviously, you will have to research many of these prices by getting hourly estimates for professional services and/or any construction work you are planning.

You may wonder why you would need some of the items listed above. Read on!

Office Supplies

Calendar/Date Book   This invaluable tool speaks for itself. The book type is best because you can carry it with you to meetings and schedule deadlines or future meetings right on the spot. Get into the habit of cross-referencing it several times a week with your family calendar. Many a meeting has been inadvertently scheduled on the same day as a child's dental appointment or a school function simply because both events weren't logged in both calendars.

Address Book/Rolodex   We also refer to this as your instant mailing list. Each time a potential client calls, enter the person's name, address, phone/fax numbers, and how he or she heard about you in your address book or onto a Rolodex card. Not only can you build up a mailing list this way; it also lets you track which marketing tools are bringing you the most responses.

Receipt Book   The more casual the type of business you operate, the more likely it is that you will be dealing with cash transactions. You must, for tax purposes, document the transaction by giving the client a cash receipt and keeping a duplicate for yourself.

Paper   You will need paper for printing, writing, fliers, copying, faxing, and simply making notes. So stock up! Make sure you throw in a couple of legal pads for good measure for note taking or just to jot down ideas as they occur to you.

Pens and Pencils   You will buy them, misplace them, lose them, leave them behind, and then find them all over again. Buy them by the case!

File Crates and Folders   You will need to store brochures, marketing information, trade magazines, contracts, and a host of other items that will take up room in your office. Stackable crates are available at most office-supply stores. They stack neatly and, at a few dollars each, are a less expensive alternative than a file cabinet.

Stapler and Staple Remover   Buy two just in case you lose one. Staples are more reliable than paper clips, less expensive overall, and will keep your important documents together.

Postal Scale   Not everyone will need one. If your business involves long-distance clients, sending heavy documents out on a regular basis, or frequent mailings, it's probably worth investing in a scale for sheer convenience. You might also want to consider leasing a postage meter if getting to the post office to buy stamps frequently is a chore.

Large Envelopes   After making a significant investment in your brochures and presentation packets you won't want them to get ruined in the mail. Large manila or white envelopes (at least nine by twelve inches) keep your material free of creases and therefore more attractive and easier to read. Purchase them in boxes of one hundred to save money.

Card File Box and Index Cards   Once you have established a relationship with a client, it's a good idea to make a "client card" to record important dates and contacts. Include birthdays, special needs the client might have, any incidents (both positive and negative) that have arisen from your working relationship, and the date of last contact. Go through your card-file box once a month to establish whom you need to call or who needs to be sent birthday greetings. Don't forget, that personal touch can set you apart from your competition. Obviously this can also be computerized with a simple database or contact-management program.

Return-Address Labels   If you have a computer and a good-quality laser or ink-jet printer, printing your own return-address labels is a snap. Boxes of labels are available at your local office-supply store; you might want to get a couple of different sizes for envelopes of various sizes you will be using. If you can't print them yourself, your local printer will be able to help you out.

Return-Address Stamp If you're on a really tight budget and don't have the equipment to print your own return-address labels, you can buy a preinked return-address stamp. This is the most economical option, but the print quality won't be as good as the alternatives. Keep an eye open for mail-order specials through Sunday circulars or in the backs of some business magazines.

Bank-Account Checks You will need checks printed for your business account. These days, you don't have to buy expensive bank checks; there are various mail-order sources that will save you money. Don't be tempted to choose an elaborate design; keep it simple and basic. If you plan on writing your checks manually, then you will need a checkbook and a supply of checks to fill it. We recommend that you purchase the larger ledger type rather than the traditional pocket checkbook. It not only will help distinguish your business checkbook from your personal books; it is simply a more organized, safer way to keep your checks. If you plan to pay all your checks with an accounting software package, then forget the book and just order the proper checks for your system.

Accounting Ledger If you don't plan to use an accounting software package, you will need to set up a manual system for keeping track of your expenditures. You will need a ledger at least ten columns across to balance your funds each month and identify where your gross income is going. The more you know about where it goes, the better you can control your expenditures and therefore keep more for your salary!

Message Pads We like the duplicate spiral-bound pads available at office-supply stores. You will have a log of all your incoming messages, which can be helpful later if you misplace a contact's telephone or fax number.

Marketing Materials

Since marketing is such an integral part of your business, you will want to spend your marketing dollars wisely and effectively and get the most mileage for your dollar. Two of your major investments early on will be in your logo (as we discussed on page 39) and a marketing brochure or other presentation piece. Although these two items may eat up most of your marketing budget, they are a sound investment, for they will keep working for you throughout the life of your business. Check around with printers for competitive pricing.

Later, in Phase III, we will show you how to put together an effective presentation folder. For now, just know that you need them. Purchased in packets of ten or more, they can cost as little as twenty-five cents a piece and will enhance your marketing-materials presentation.

Professional Services

Budget at least $250 for consultations with an attorney and an accountant, which can be a bargain if you go prepared with a list of specific questions. Sometimes you can arrange for a brief initial consultation that is free of charge, so shop around. The more information you are able to obtain gratis, the more you will have left over to spend on marketing.You'll need to talk to your insurance agent about adding a rider to your current policy. Ask how much liability and property insurance he or she feels your business needs. Usually, a rider can be added to your current insurance and may only raise it by a few dollars per year. You may be pleasantly surprised at how little it costs to protect your business. Learn more about insurance in Chapter 6.

Finding the Funds

So, what's the next step once you have figured out how much you need? Finding the funds, of course. Unfortunately, there is no magic wand you can wave and have the money fall in your lap! But you have some options. Consider them and then decide what is best for you. Keep in mind that it will be the responsibility of your business to pay back any loans it receives.

■ *Borrow from a savings account.* Start-up costs for a home-based business can run from less than five hundred dollars for a modest beginning all the way up to ten thousand dollars or more (for the works!). Your home office will probably fall somewhere in between. Not everyone has three, four, or five thousand dollars lying around in an accessible savings account just waiting to be spent. And we don't recommend cashing in the kids' college fund or absorbing hefty penalties by eating away at an IRA or 401K plan (although you may wish to use them as collateral).

■ *Borrow from relatives.* Many a successful business was started because family and friends believed in an idea and backed it. If you do borrow from your family, however, approach doing so as you would any business transaction. Draw up a contract that specifies the amount borrowed; interest on the loan, if any; and the repayment schedule. If you run into difficulty making payments on time, go to your relatives before they come to you and let them know what the situation is. Presumably, they will work with you to make the payment schedule more affordable. Whatever else you do, don't feel that you don't have to take the loan seriously because it's only Aunty Jane's money. That's not fair to her, and you will lose credibility with her and probably all your other relatives, too.

■ *Don't fund your business with credit cards.* Sure, we've all heard of those success stories about businesses that were started by maxing out the credit cards, but doing so could backfire on you badly. Don't forget, the interest rate on credit cards is incredibly high, so unless you are absolutely sure that you will be able to pay off your balances within a very short period of time, find the money somewhere else.

■ *Approach your bank—with some trepidation—for a business loan.* Historically, banks have not been particularly interested in the home-based-business market. As a woman, you will probably have another strike against you. Still, it's worth a try. Assuming you have good credit, a reasonable debt-to-income ratio, and a solid business plan, talk to your bank about obtaining a loan.

A bank can stretch a loan over a period of several years so that your payments will be affordable while you build your credit as a business owner in the process. You can always prepay your loan (check first to see if there are any penalties for prepayment) if your business takes off quickly and you would rather be debt-free. Plus, if you decide to expand, invest in a new computer or additional office equipment, or even build a larger office in your home, your history of steady, on-time payments against the initial loan will predispose your bank to look at future loan applications much more favorably.

Impressing the Bank

Your initial visit to the bank will be a very important one. After all, first impressions can be key in lasting relationships. By following the simple rules listed below, you can give yourself a much better chance of walking out with a loan:

■ *Dress the part.* Don't wander into the bank in your favorite worn jeans with two or three kids in tow between trips to the grocery store and the dry cleaner. You won't be taken seriously. Dress professionally, hire a sitter, and go prepared with a well-thought-out and well-rehearsed presentation.

■ *Go armed with a business plan.* This could be simply a few pages about your business, your qualifications to run your business, and an income-projection sheet detailing how your business will make money. The more money you ask for, the more supporting documentation you will need. (Information on writing a successful business plan is available through the Small Business Administration (SBA) or see our Resources section for suggestions on books to help you write a business plan.)

■ *Start with the bank you use for your personal checking and savings accounts.* This will make it much easier for you if you already have a good track record with the bank.

■ *Have a backup plan.* As we mentioned earlier, it is unfortunate but true that banks have been slow to recognize that many successful businesses are being started from home. There is still a perception that home-based businesses are a poor financial risk, but as the industry continues to grow, eventually financial institutions will start actively marketing to this booming population. In the meantime, if

What If the Bank Doesn't Want to Lend You Money?

If you have not had a loan before and the bank feels you are a risk, ask the loan officer if you can use your savings or retirement fund as collateral. Or perhaps they will accept your application if someone cosigns your loan. This can be a parent, your husband, or someone close to you who is prepared to back you. Once you have had a loan and been successful paying it back, you will be able to obtain unsecured loans much more easily.

If you have no collateral and know of no one who can cosign for you, consider the SBA loan guarantee program. Unfortunately, the SBA's funding has been cut in recent years, and obtaining a loan can be a tortuous process, but if you have no other options, it may be worth trying. You will need a well-written business plan, and you will have to wade through their paperwork, but your effort could bring you an SBA-guaranteed loan. This means that if you should default on the loan, the SBA will repay the bank on your behalf.

you are denied a business loan, request a personal loan instead. Often business owners who have gone in for a business loan and been unsuccessful have been easily approved for a personal loan and used those funds for their business. If you have good credit and a history of paying credit cards, car payments, and mortgage payments on time, then you should be a good candidate for a personal loan.

- *Request enough but not too much!* Don't bite off more than you can chew by applying for several thousand more than you really need. You may be setting yourself up for a hefty payment each month that you'll find tough to meet. Try to keep your monthly payments at a reasonable, *affordable* amount.

Choosing a Bank for Your Business

The criteria you use when choosing a bank for your business account need be no different than those you consider when selecting other service providers you will deal with on a regular basis. For example, the grocery store you use the most is probably the one that is most conveniently located, is open at the right times, and combines optimum product choice with service efficiency and good prices. When you choose a bank, you'll want to look for these same qualities.

These days you can usually find a bank at every major intersection, in every shopping mall, and they are even popping up in grocery stores and office buildings. Each one is focused on getting your money into their vaults, and they know they have lots of competition. Longer hours, lower interest rates on loans, interest-bearing checking accounts, free checking, and ATMs (automated teller machines) are just a few of the many services a bank can provide.

If you decide to look for a new bank for your business account, you will probably find it easiest to get out the yellow pages and start calling around. Let the bank know that you want to open a business account and ask about the special services they offer to business customers. Here are some questions you can ask to determine if a bank will suit your needs:

- Is there a monthly fee for checking-account services? If so, what is that fee?
- Is there an additional charge for each check written?
- Do they offer overdraft protection?
- How do they handle checks which are returned to you from your clients due to insufficient funds? (i.e., do they charge you, too?)
- Do they offer a free ATM card?
- If so, is there a fee per transaction from an ATM?
- Do they grant small-business loans? At what interest rate?
- What are their drive-through and lobby hours? (Ask yourself if their hours are convenient for your lifestyle.)

- Do they return your checks with the monthly statement? (Some banks will keep your checks and store them on microfiche instead of sending them back to you at the end of each month. In the event of an audit, you will need your checks.)
- Do they pay interest on checking accounts?

Once you have collected this information, you should be able to narrow your list down to a few banks that will best meet your business needs. The next step is to make an appointment to visit the various banks and determine who offers the best in service (first and foremost), location, and convenience.

After you have made your decision, make a point of introducing yourself to the bank manager and the assistant managers. If a problem arises, you won't want to waste time and energy on introductions before you can get your problem solved. Also, you may want to consider moving your personal accounts to the same bank. Running around town to different banks for personal and business use is a waste of time and annoying. (Not to mention what all those free lollipops do to your children's teeth!)

Obtaining Merchant Status

Obtaining merchant status allows you to accept credit-card payments from your customers. The convenience of this payment option will be appreciated by your customers—especially if you do a lot of mail-order, trade show, or telephone sales—and sometimes will clinch a sale you might otherwise have lost. Unfortunately, banks are more reluctant to grant merchant status (the ability to process credit-card transactions) to home-based businesses because of the higher potential for fraud when credit transactions are made primarily over the phone or via fax—the way most home-based businesses operate. For this reason, a home-based business will usually be held to a higher credit standard than other applicants and may have to endure an arduous process before obtaining approval.

Bank-Information Work Sheet

Name of bank _____

Location of bank _____

Phone number _____

Type of bank (credit union, savings and loan, etc.) _____

1. Is there a monthly fee for business-checking-account services? _____
    If yes, what is it for? _____

2. Is there an additional charge for each check written? _____
    If yes, how much? _____

3. Does the bank offer overdraft protection? _____

4. How do they handle checks returned from clients due to insufficient funds? (i.e., do
    they charge you, too?) _____

5. Do they offer a free ATM card?

6. How much do they charge for ATM transactions? _____

7. Do they grant small-business loans? _____ What is the current interest rate
    charged? _____

8. The lobby hours are Monday–Friday _____
    Saturday _____

9. The drive through hours are Monday–Friday _____
    Saturday _____

10. Do they return your checks with the monthly statement? _____ (Some banks
    will keep your checks and store them on microfiche instead of sending them back to
    you each month. In the event of an IRS audit, you will need your checks.)

11. On a scale of 1 to 10, I found the customer service, attitude, and professionalism while
    conducting this initial interview to be: _____

12. On a scale of 1 to 10, I would rate the overall service and convenience of this bank to
    be: _____

But doing this isn't impossible, as Sherri Breetzke, owner of www.creativityzone.com, an Internet retailing business, found. "I had to supply all the usual information included on their standard application form: address, type of business, business hours, state sales tax ID number, date of birth, and social security number, etc. I also had to provide three references—people who had done business with the Creativity Zone—to prove that I was a real business. They also wanted to see a copy of my occupational license and copies of my business cards and brochure.

"The bank then sent an 'investigator' to my house to ensure that there really was an office set up at the address I gave them on my application. Finally, I had to fill out a 'Merchant Profile Analysis.' This is where I got into trouble because of one of the questions that was asked: "Explain where inventory is kept." I don't keep any inventory; I just process orders and send the invoices to the suppliers to fill. Based on my response to this question, I was initially turned down for merchant status."

Not about to be deterred, Sherri offered additional information to the bank that elaborated on her business practices and proved that while she didn't have a "physical" inventory on the premises, she kept a detailed computerized inventory and was running a serious operation. Finally, the bank gave her the go-ahead, and Sherri was ready to take orders. Her advice for others seeking merchant status?

- *Plan ahead.* It's going to take a while, and you need to anticipate and be prepared to regroup if your application is declined the first time around.

- *Do all your homework first.* Set up your business checking account, obtain your state-tax ID number, have your business/ occupational license, establish some business contacts (even just someone who prints your business cards), be able to show some advertising, and preferably have an advertising agreement to show you are actively promoting your business.

Costs involved probably vary from bank to bank. You can generally expect an up-front application fee plus an advance payment on the equipment lease. Then you'll have a monthly lease fee for equipment/software, etc., plus a fee for each credit-card transaction.

Is It Worth It?

For Sherri, and others whose businesses depend on their ability to offer credit transactions to customers, the answer is a resounding Yes! Sherri's story is yet another example of how persistence can pay off for the home-based entrepreneur.

Knowing Where Your Money Goes

Once you have chosen your bank, established a checking account, and ordered your checks and deposit slips, you will need to perfect a method for keeping track of what's coming in and what's going out. There are at least two ways to accomplish this.

First, if you have a personal computer, we recommend a basic accounting software program. Not only will this keep all your records organized and at your fingertips, but you can also print reports that show you instantly where every penny of your business income is going. Reconciling your account with your bank statement each month can be accomplished in a matter of minutes. It's also more impressive to pull out a couple of computer-generated reports when you are shopping for financial assistance. For less than fifty dollars you should be able to pick up a software package that will more than meet your needs.

Our second suggestion, and only for those who do not plan to use a computer for their business, is to use a manual ledger. This method, like the accounting software, will keep track of your funds—how much comes in, how much goes out, and where it all goes. Both methods get you the same results. The difference is in the additional time you spend on a manual system. If you need to use the manual method, make sure you purchase a ledger with at least ten columns and assign a category to each of the following:

- Deposit
- Withdrawal
- Salary
- Advertising and postage
- Telephone/long distance
- Travel and entertainment
- Accounting and legal fees
- Office supplies
- Other equipment
- Insurance

You may decide you need a ledger with even more columns to ensure that you cover all the categories you want to include. Don't forget that the less you spend in other areas, the more you can carry over into that very important category marked salary! Balance your ledger at least monthly when your bank statement comes in, then close out each month and carry the beginning figures over into the new month. By keeping careful accounting records, tax time will be easier, and you'll have an ongoing gauge of your financial progress. If you make less in March than you did in February, you might want to analyze what you did differently, if anything. Obviously, your business, like any other, will be subject to fluctuations, but keeping on top of it will let you see if it's a minor change or a trend to be concerned about.

If you see no progress or a decline in growth, perhaps you need to beef up your marketing efforts. On the other hand, if things are going gangbusters you may need to review your ability to handle your growing workload. But you won't know this unless you do your checks and balances on a regular basis. The practice itself is not fun, but the result can be. Especially if the news is encouraging!

The information in this chapter, along with guidance from the financial institution you choose to work with, should help you tremendously in understanding how your money works and *should* work for you. Don't be afraid to ask questions of your banker; it is your job to become educated on what options you have, just as it is in the banker's interest to help your business succeed. Remember, the more you know about the financial status of your business, the more you can do to keep it growing. You can bank on it!

6

Your Legal Options and Responsibilities

You will quickly discover that becoming a business owner brings with it certain responsibilities. It is up to you to find out what licenses, permits, or other paperwork are required on a local, state, or even national level and to make sure that your business is in compliance. You'll also want to make sure that you have adequate insurance for your new business and, if appropriate, legal protection in the form of incorporation. Don't worry: it's not nearly as time-consuming as it sounds!

Zoning Permits and Business Licenses

If life were easy, there would be no such thing as business licenses, zoning laws, or building permits. Anyone could choose to start a business—any business—buy a neon sign, and set up shop right in their own front yard. Thank heaven for business licenses, zoning laws, and building permits!

Although life would be simpler without yet another trip to the local government office to obtain approval for the business you want to start from home, it is precisely these ordinances that protect us all. Without them, the guy down the street might be able to run a pool hall out of his basement, or that kooky retired schoolteacher could put up a flashing multicolored sign in her front yard offering tea-leaf and palm readings.

The first thing you need to know is that these ordinances are very specific to the town, county, subdivision, or jurisdiction in which you live. In some parts of the country the regulations are very favorable because local officials see the benefits in promoting and encouraging home-based business start-ups. Many others, however, make it more difficult. You should start by checking any covenants that govern the subdivision or condo in which you live. Some of these prohibit operating a business out of a home, and you may need to apply for a special-use permit.

Your second stop will be the local zoning office. In many cases it is just a matter of the office issuing a zoning permit to allow you to run a business out of your home. The simpler your business, the less you will need to worry about. But if you need specialized equipment to run your business or if you will have clients coming to your home regularly, you may need to go before the zoning board for approval before they will issue a permit. Waiting for them to consider your request can be a tedious process—made worse by the fact that most zoning boards only meet monthly or quarterly. Sometimes the board will invite your neighbors to attend these meetings; if they have objections to your plans, your application will be denied.

The key to fast approval is tailoring your business to fit that simple home-based business mold. How do you keep it simple?

- *Plan to meet clients somewhere other than your home.* Although there may be times when it is absolutely essential that clients come to your home office, do not make it a regular habit. It is the zoning board's job to protect your neighbors from excessive traffic that may be caused by a business in your community.

- *Do not display a sign anywhere on the property.* The zoning board will consider a sign as a possible eyesore to your neighbors and the community and will probably require board approval.

■ *Do not plan on building a warehouse out back to store a huge inventory.* If you must have some inventory on the premises, keep it within reason. If you plan on designing T-shirts, do not have a Fruit of the Loom truck back up in your driveway and drop off a hundred thousand shirts. Consider storage space you already have, convert a closet, or if you need much more room, rent a storage space nearby.

■ *Accept your limitations.* Some businesses just aren't suitable for a residential neighborhood. Any business that requires use of noisy equipment, industrial supplies, or heavy-duty machinery is better located in commercial office space.

Once you have your permit, you will need to obtain a business license (renewed annually) for a nominal fee. This fee will vary if, as in some areas, it is based on a percentage of your gross income. Once you obtain your business license, you will be registered for business in the community.

Note: Do not confuse obtaining a business license with registration with the U.S. Patent Trademark Office. Your name is not registered nationally and has no trade name or trademark protection when simply registered at the county level.

Don't forget, if you plan to build on to your home, any build-out will require a builder's permit. If you are using a contractor to do the work, he will be responsible for obtaining the permits. But if you are planning to do the work yourself, don't forget to apply for the appropriate permits first.

In some areas of the country, such as rural areas with very limited local government, there are no restrictions on home-based businesses, and in some not even a license is required. This isn't the norm, however. If, after careful research, you can find no license or zoning regulations in your area, you should assume that you can set up your business without one. Just to be safe, you might want to check with one or two local established businesses to confirm that no license is required.

Should You Use Your Home Address?

Not all home-based business owners choose to use their home address as the business address, preferring instead to rent a mail box at the local post office or other facility.

There's no right or wrong, but there are advantages and disadvantages to each approach. Consider the following before you make your decision:

Using Home Address versus	*Renting a Mailing Address*
Pros	Cons
Convenient for receiving mail	Inconvenient—requires trip out.
No additional cost	Fees for renting a P.O. Box are $15 and up
Cons	Pros
More difficult to separate personal mail from business correspondence	Easier to keep mail separate (and out of the kids' hands!)
Advertises the fact that you have business equipment at this location	Home address is unknown to general public
If you move, you must change address on all your business stationery and brochures	If you move locally, you can still use the same business address
If address sounds residential (e.g., Weeping Willow Way, Shady Grove Court), it's a tip that you're home-based!	If address is a P.O. box, it's a tip that you're home-based!

Insurance

Most people wouldn't dream of being without home, auto, or life insurance. Yet many home-based business owners don't insure their home-based businesses. This can backfire in the event of a house fire or other catastrophe because your office computer, copier, and other business supplies and assets may not be covered.

Imagine coming home from a family vacation to find that your home was burglarized and ransacked in your absence. Missing? A computer system valued at three thousand dollars, a personal copier valued at one thousand dollars, televisions, a stereo, a VCR, some jewelry, and credit cards. After reporting the loss to your insurance company, you learn that the computer and copier will not be covered simply because they don't belong to your home; they belong to your business. *And you never took out additional insurance for your business*. This kind of loss can be devastating to a small business, and it may take months to pull together the resources to replace the stolen items. In the meantime, your business suffers.

An equally unthinkable but even scarier scenario would be to have one of your clients visit you at home to work on a project, fall down your front step, and break a few bones in the process. If this person decides to sue you for damages, loss of work, and medical expenses, guess what? Under most homeowner's policies a claim like this would not be covered unless you had added an insurance rider to cover any liability related to your business.

Our advice, before you take another step toward opening your business, is to contact your insurance agent and get an estimate for adding appropriate insurance coverage. This should include fire, flood, lost wages due to catastrophe, burglary, liability, and even contract insurance. Remember, there is no such thing as being overinsured when it comes to protecting your business. The additional fee may pinch a little, but you'll benefit not only from peace of mind but also, in the event of a disaster, replacements!

A Personal Glimpse As the founder and president of the American Association of Home-Based Business, Beverley Williams strongly recommends additional insurance coverage for home-based business owners, in part because she *almost* had to learn the hard way. When she first started her desktop publishing and design business, she assumed that her existing homeowner's insurance policy would also cover any equipment she used in her work. But when a cracked second-floor storm window shattered, showering broken glass below, Beverley realized that she could have been held liable had a client been standing there at the time. On checking with her insurance agent, she discovered that, in fact, she had no liability coverage for that type of accident. If a client were injured, it would be regarded as a "business situation," and as such not covered under a homeowner's policy. She was also informed that none of her valuable electronic equipment was covered for damage or loss, either.

Needless to say, Beverley immediately purchased a policy to cover all her business activities. The timing was extremely fortunate. Only months later, a violent thunderstorm blew out much of the wiring in her home, along with all her computer equipment, fax, and copier. A single lightning strike wiped out equipment worth ten thousand dollars. Her recently acquired insurance policy enabled her to replace everything. Beverley's advice? Don't wait to buy additional insurance. The couple of hundred dollars you will spend on the policy might save you from total disaster later on.

Should You Incorporate?

"Should I incorporate my business?" Unfortunately, this question ranks right up there with "Should I get a root canal?" Pleasant? No. Necessary? Maybe. There is nothing about incorporating your business that is easy, fun, or enticing unless you enjoy implementing bylaws, conducting shareholders' meetings with yourself, and keeping track of minutes. The one big advantage is protection. Incorporating your business provides personal protection that even insurance won't match.

Here's how it works. When you build a business as a sole

proprietor, you and the business are one and the same in the eyes of the world. The downside is that you, as the sole proprietor, will be personally responsible for any claims against your business. This means that if your business is sued or owes a debt or taxes, the world outside can dip right into your personal pockets to claim the money owed and you cannot stop them. But if you are incorporated, your business is a separate entity, and you are merely an employee of that entity. The business stands on its own, pays its own debts, and answers for its own liabilities. You just work for it.

Now, if your business is quite simple, its anticipated income is less than fifty thousand dollars annually, and you are not at high risk of experiencing a large debt, tax, or lawsuit, then a sole proprietorship may be just what the doctor ordered. But consider the following: You will see that you can't always predict what can go wrong, and for a business owner, that can have dire consequences.

When Kim left work to be home with her two toddlers, she decided to start a business that would help with the monthly bills while also giving her a sense of self beyond being just Kevin and Rebecca's mom. Kim had always loved weddings—she had particularly enjoyed planning her own—and was sure she could succeed as a professional wedding planner. As Kim rounded up vendors, put together marketing material, and researched caterers, she knew she had made the right decision. She was having fun, working a manageable fifteen to twenty hours each week, and she looked forward to the time she spent with the brides-to-be and their families.

All was going well until one gloomy Saturday morning in May when she had a lavish outdoor wedding planned for 3:00 P.M. Kim realized as soon as she woke up that the weather wasn't going to cooperate and that rain was imminent. The wedding would have to take place under a tent or run the risk of being a washout.

She quickly called a tent rental company she frequently used and told them to make sure that they delivered and erected a tent before noon. At 2:30 P.M., Kim was in a state of panic when there was still no tent to be found, and despite repeated attempts she couldn't reach anyone at the rental company. At 3:05 P.M. the rain arrived, drenching the bride, groom, guests, food, and of course, Kim. At least no one could see the tears streaming down her cheeks.

First thing Monday morning, Kim received a call from the newlyweds' attorney informing her that the devastated couple were going to file a lawsuit. The rental company claimed that they never had received Kim's call about the tent, so she was on her own to fight the battle. When all was said and done, Kim was found liable and therefore responsible for repaying ten thousand dollars to the families. Needless to say, a fine of that magnitude put her out of business for good and forced Kim and her husband to remortgage their house to pay the debt. Kim closed her business and went back to office work to help pay the additional mortgage payments.

If Kim had incorporated, the liability would have rested with the corporation. If the corporation had been found guilty of negligence, the penalty would not have reached Kim's personal pocketbook and affected her and her family so greatly. Would the corporation still have been responsible for the debt? Yes, but since the corporation's assets would be limited, the plaintiff would have no choice but to accept a payment schedule that was convenient and realistic for the corporation.You might think that your business just doesn't warrant the hassles of incorporating, and it may seem more trouble than it's worth. But it does provide an invaluable safety net in case of trouble. As you decide whether or not to take this step, consider *any* and *every* possible scenario related to your business that could cause you liability. If even the slightest possibility of accident, injury, or liability exists, you should incorporate to protect yourself and your family.

There are countless guides to incorporating a business, and if you are not too intimidated by the process, you may be able to incorporate your business yourself—without using an attorney. Most well-equipped office-supply stores carry do-it-yourself kits containing the information you need to incorporate in your state. A kit should include forms, directions, and an explanation about the benefits of incorporating and the type of corporation that will best suit your needs. If you are more comfortable with an attorney

---

What *Type* of Corporation Should You Opt For?

There are two types of corporations. One is the regular corporation, or C corporation, the other is the subchapter, or S corporation. We find that for a small business the S corporation is a much simpler type of corporation to run. The main difference between an S Corp and a C Corp is the rate at which your business is taxed. They both, however, provide the liability protection you need.

Our recommendation? Use the funds you budgeted for legal and accounting fees to consult with a tax accountant and get guidance on whether you should incorporate and, if so, which type of corporation makes the most sense for your business.

---

handling the procedure for you, once again, shop around, as prices vary. The smaller the law office, usually the lower the fee for preparing the incorporation papers.

Should You File a Registered Trademark?

We have mentioned trademarking frequently so far in this book, and with good reason. Many small-business owners don't bother to trademark because they assume that as a small hometown business they won't need the protection a trademark provides. But you can't guarantee that no one else will want to use the name you have picked, and if that company does choose to trademark, you are in trouble.

For example, the Fresh Bakery in LittleTown, U.S.A., has been in business for three years delivering lunchtime sandwiches and other baked goods to local businesses. Since their business is purely local, they never think to register the name. Out of the blue, they receive a registered letter from the legal department of Corporation X—a large national corporation. The letter states that this company has registered the name the Fresh Bakery with the U.S. Patent and

Trademark Office with the sole intention of using the name to market its new line of breakfast pastries. Who wins? The one who got to the U.S. Patent and Trademark Office first. And so the Fresh Bakery in LittleTown is left with only two options: It must either reestablish itself under a new name in town—absorbing the cost of changing its menus, preprinted paper bags, and other printed materials—or, face a possible lawsuit or close its doors. Neither choice is very appealing.

When you think of it in those terms, the three hundred dollars or so that it costs to trademark seems like small change for the protection that will keep the name of your business safe from infringement.

7

Your Business Policies and Procedures

You know the questions because as a consumer you've asked them. "How much do you charge? Do you take checks? How late are you open? Can you hold this for three days? Does that come with a guarantee? When will this be ready to pick up?"

Consumers like to know what to expect from a business. It's smart to establish a set of policies and procedures so that you are not caught off guard when a customer asks a question about your business practices.

It is up to you how you actually set your policies. If you want to reserve Fridays as a catch-up day, for example, make sure your customers know that you are only available between Monday and Thursday. If your bank, like most, charges you when a customer bounces a check, attach a fee of twenty-five dollars for each returned check to cover your own costs and discourage careless clients from doing this. If you don't want to deal with accounts receivable and billing cycles, make sure you tell clients that you must be paid in full at the time of delivery of the product or service ordered. You should build your policies and procedures around what you want to do and how you want to set up and organize your daily operations.

Your Pricing Policy

"How much?" It's one of the first questions most of us ask when considering a purchase, and now that you're in business, you'll hear the question often, too. You can't run a business successfully without establishing a pricing policy—one based on what you are selling, what your market will bear, how much profit you want to make, and how much your competition charges. The way you calculate your pricing structure will depend on whether you are selling a product or offering a service.

Pricing A Product

If you sell a product, you will have a starting point—either the wholesale cost of the product plus an appropriate markup for overhead or, if you manufacture your products, the cost of raw materials and labor, with a markup to cover overhead.

For example, Jane makes and sells felt hats for babies and toddlers. She is able to produce thirty hats each week. Jane's total cost of materials for one week's worth of hats, including fabric, thread, and notions, is $25. She wants to pay herself at least $100 each week. (If she were using hired help, she would need to factor in staff wages too.) So her total cost for raw materials and labor is $125 for one week's production of thirty hats. Now she needs to add the cost of her weekly overhead (includes marketing materials, insurance, packing materials, shipping costs, telephone, insurance, equipment maintenance, office supplies, etc.). She has calculated her monthly overhead at $160 per month, which translates to $40 per week. This brings her total costs for the week to $165. Her total production is thirty hats, which gives her a cost of $5.50 per hat.

To arrive at a selling price, Jane must decide on how much profit she wants to make from each hat and add that, too. She wants to make $3.00 per hat and adds this to the $5.50 each hat costs to produce for a final selling price of $8.50 per hat—the price she must charge to meet the income and profit criteria she has set.

Pricing a Product

Costs for one week's production of felt hats—thirty hats.

1. Cost of direct materials felt, notions, thread		$ 25
2. Cost of labor your salary		$100
3. Cost of overhead		$ 40
TOTAL		**$165**
	Total direct cost per hat = $165/30 hats =	$5.50 per hat
4. Add the profit you want to make		$3.00 per hat
TOTAL SELLING PRICE		**$8.50 per hat**

Pricing a Service

If you are in a service business, your labor will generally be the major portion of your pricing formula. You will either charge a flat hourly rate or calculate your charges on a per-project basis. Obviously, this is less cut-and-dried than pricing a product, because you don't have a basis to start from, so it is easy to miscalculate the fees you need to charge to make a profit. As a home-based business, you will typically have an advantage over your local non-home-based competition because your overhead will be much lower and you can pass the savings on to your clients. But even though it is tempting to offer cut-rate prices—especially when you are trying to get your foot in the door—setting your prices too low can be as bad for your business as setting them too high.

Prospective customers don't consider only price when making a buying decision. Obviously, they want to be assured of quality service, too. If your prices are too low, they might assume that your service is similarly cut-rate.

Underpricing can also backfire later on when you want to pursue higher-end jobs. Even though you offer excellent service and do really good work, you may find that you have firmly established yourself as a "lower-cost" option and you aren't being considered for the more lucrative opportunities. It's always better to price yourself at the right level to start with and offer a "new customer discount" to win the first piece of business and establish a relationship. Just make sure your new client realizes that it is a one-time-only price and that any future jobs will be done at your regular fee.

A *Personal Glimpse* How do you know if your price is right? What if *some* people grumble about your prices? According to Peggy Shaffer, who runs a tax and accounting business from her home, "You know your prices are too low if everyone says, 'Wow, your prices are great!' But you know you are right on target when maybe 5 percent of your potential clients complain. If *no one* complains, you're pricing yourself too low."

Peggy established her own fee schedule by working backward. Her starting point was the annual income she wanted to make and the number of hours she wanted to work. She then factored in the length of time it would take her to accomplish each task, took into account how much her competition was charging, and set her rates accordingly. From this she drew up an itemized price list, which she adjusts every other year to cover her increased overhead.

Peggy can afford to price herself competitively and still make a profit because she doesn't have the large staff and huge overhead that large accounting firms must factor in to their fee schedule. She has met and surpassed her original income goals for herself while still enjoying a manageable workload and time with her son. She knows what her time and expertise are worth, and experience has taught her that it's not usually worth haggling over price. "The people who want to talk you down from what you know is a *fair price* are the biggest pains. They won't be happy whatever you do and in the end will still find a reason to complain."

However you set your prices, you will need to make sure your clients are aware of them as early as possible. This prevents any misunderstandings. By presenting them with your price list or fee structure in your list of policies and procedures, you give them the information up front and the opportunity to ask any questions at that time.

Turnaround Time

It's going to be hard to get your pricing right if you are way off when estimating the time a specific project will take you. When you first start your business, you will probably find that your estimates aren't always accurate, but experience will help you do better. As a rule of thumb, if you're not sure, always estimate more time than you think you'll need. This will give you a comfortable margin of error so that you won't lose money or compromise quality by rushing if the job takes longer than you expected. Your customers also need to be told how long it will take you to complete their job or fulfill their order.

Let's say you decide to use your crafting talents to start a wreath-making business. You visit a client, coordinate her colors, and together you choose the flowers you will use in the wreath. Three days later, your client calls you and asks when she can pick up her wreath. Unfortunately, you're not yet a third of the way finished. The client may have been totally unrealistic to call so soon, but if she had been told up front that the lead time on her order would be at least two weeks, she would not have expected it to be ready before then.

If worse comes to worst and you know you are not going to be able to deliver on time, notify the client as soon as you can. Don't wait for the delivery date to pass and the client to call you demanding to know where the job is. Your client may not be pleased but will appreciate the fact that you gave her some advance warning.

When estimating the time it will take you to complete a project:

▪ Make your best estimate and then add half as much time again. It's always acceptable to deliver earlier than agreed but unprofessional to deliver later than promised.

▪ Take into account your current workload; you don't want to neglect projects you may already be working on.

▪ Remember Murphy's home-based-moms rule number two: your children always get sick when you are at your busiest! Have a backup plan in case this happens.

▪ If you cannot avoid missing a deadline with a client, call apologetically and let the person know. Never miss a deadline with that client again; once is enough.

Your policies and procedures should also address and clarify the following:

Payment Schedules   Making clients aware of your payment policy is a must in any type of business. By putting your policy in writing and presenting it up front, you can avoid questions, confusion, and negotiations over how you should be paid.

When you pick up your dry cleaning, you pay the fee for the service; you don't expect to have the option to be billed later or "run a tab." The policy is clear becuase it was presented to you the first time you entered, either on the claim slip or on the counter near the register. You should do the same thing. Put your payment policy in writing and make sure your clients read and understand it. Then, for the sake of consistency, stick to it!

Some businesses offer a range of payment options to established customers, but it may not be convenient for you to issue invoices or accept payments on installment. Most small home-based businesses operate best with a policy of immediate payment. In some cases, you might want to ask for a deposit when you begin work, with the balance payable upon completion.

Guarantees or Refunds   It is difficult to have a refund policy on a service, for there is nothing tangible for the client to return in order to obtain that refund. However, by stating a guarantee policy—that you will make every effort to satisfy the client—you are assuring your clients that they will get their money's worth.

Hours of Operation This is a must when you work from home because you never leave the office, really. Let's say you decide to establish work hours from 9:30 A.M. to 4:00 P.M., Monday through Thursday. During these hours, clients may contact you by phone, set up appointments with you, or obtain your product or service. These hours are convenient for you because by 9:30 A.M. the kids are fed and dressed and the baby is ready for his morning nap. By the end of your "official" workday, at 4:00 P.M., you are thinking about dinner and preparing for some family time before you play catch-up in your office later. By setting these hours, you know you can safely ignore the business phone when it rings outside of this time frame. Make sure, though, that you specify your hours on the outgoing message of your answering machine or voice mail. This way, if clients reach your message after your regular hours, they won't expect a call back until the next business day.

Incentives One of your best marketing tools is a happy client. Give your customers incentive to pass the word on about your business and they will! Offering incentives, such as a discount or coupon for a free product or service, is one way to say thank you for referrals. But make sure they know about your incentive practice by listing it in your policies and procedures. Don't be too stingy, either; make it worth your busy clients' time to refer you.

Waivers of Liability Let your clients know what you are responsible for and what you are not responsible for. The sign in the locker room at your favorite health club states that they are not responsible for items left unattended. The local indoor children's playground states that they are not responsible for injuries sustained while on the equipment. The swimming pool in your neighborhood posts a Swim at Your Own Risk sign when a lifeguard is not on duty. These are all ways of relieving the business or facility of liability when a problem occurs. Your liability will vary depending on the type of business you are running. Consult your attorney when writing your "waivers." You'll want to make sure you have considered and addressed all possible scenarios.

Inclement-Weather Policy You don't want to be faced with risking your personal safety or that of your children by making deliveries or meeting clients when the weather is bad. If this is likely to be an issue for you, include a provision stating that your business will not operate if the roads are dangerous because of severe weather conditions.

These are just some of the policies and procedures that you should address on your sheet; you may have more that are unique to your business. Don't make it too lengthy, though; keeping it to one sheet of paper will save you copying expenses, and your clients will be more inclined to read it.

Your Contract

We've all seen them, read them, and signed them at some time in our lives. A written contract can be a paragraph, a page, or several pages. By definition, it is an agreement enforceable by law. It serves both the presenter and the recipient of the contract. It creates a commitment that is more than just a frame of mind; it is a tangible item that is read, understood, and must be abided by. Every business should have one.

Even the smallest, simplest businesses benefit from a written document that spells out the business's responsibilities to its clients and the responsibilities of the clients in return. A contract doesn't have to be complicated and filled with legal jargon; it can be simply a one-page agreement or even just a paragraph at the end of a policies-and-procedures sheet that your client signs to signify that he has read, understood, and agreed to all the provisions stated.

Basically, a contract is the way that two or more parties spell out the terms of their working relationship. It addresses the responsibilities of each party to each other as well as policies, payment schedules, liability waivers, guarantees, and refunds.

Let's say that Susan starts a desktop publishing business specializing in the design of brochures, fliers, and other marketing pieces for small businesses. She contacts several local printers to introduce her new business to them, hoping that they will subcontract her to do some design work. Several printers express interest, and Susan is confident that her strategy will pay off.

Within days, Susan gets a call from ABC Printers, which has been hired to print a brochure for their new client, a florist shop. Since ABC doesn't have a designer on staff, it asks Susan to design and produce a camera-ready draft. She promptly produces an attractive, well-designed brochure, sends it to the printer with an invoice for her time, and moves on to her next project. Weeks go by, and still there is no check from ABC Printers. Susan calls to find out why she hasn't been paid and is told that although the clients were pleased with the design, they were unhappy with the print quality of the brochure, and are refusing to pay ABC's bill. As a result, ABC hasn't paid Susan, even though she fulfilled her obligation. Susan is understandably upset because she is paying the price for the printer's error even though she did what she was supposed to do.

This whole messy situation could have been avoided if Susan had first asked the printer to sign a simple agreement stating that Susan was a subcontractor to ABC Printers, whom she would invoice for her work. As the contractor, ABC would be liable for Susan's invoice *whether or not they were paid by their client*. Instead, Susan is stuck with an unpaid invoice and a ruined relationship with the printer. She also knows it could cost her more to take the matter to court than to just write it off as a loss.

Susan didn't need a complicated document to spell out the relationship between her business and ABC Printers, and it would have saved her time and money. In other situations, a more complex document might be necessary, in which case it probably makes sense to involve an attorney. If you still want to "do it yourself," invest some time in research before you start. Study other contracts and make notes on the issues addressed and the verbiage used, and then have an attorney review your work. If you opt to have an attorney draft your contract from scratch, make sure you go prepared with a list of any items specific to your business that need to be covered. It is then the attorney's job to write the language in such a way that each point is adequately covered and your best interests have been served.

Read your contract carefully to make sure it provides adequate protection and meets all your criteria. Ask a trusted friend to review the contract as a potential client and give you feedback on it. Revise it until you are satisfied with it.

Once you have a contract, always take one with you when you meet with a prospective client. This way, if you win the business, you won't have to schedule another meeting just to sign an agreement. Having the document with you allows you to present it, sign it, and begin working on their job immediately. If there are clauses the client is uncomfortable with, you have the opportunity to negotiate there and then.

One last note about agreements and contracts—make certain the language used comes as close as possible to common everyday language. No client wants to pay extra for an attorney to translate your agreement to them. If you have an attorney draw up your contracts, make sure they know of your preference early on. You don't want to pay for something that makes no sense to you or anyone who hasn't had years of legal training!

Negotiating Successfully

Belinda spent countless hours working on a proposal and contract for a potential client who was considering hiring her to run several sales-training seminars over the following twelve months. It was the break she had been waiting for—a long-term, lucrative contract that could lead to other opportunities. Thus, when her client balked at some of the clauses in her contract, she immediately acquiesced and made the changes in the client's favor, although doing so would cut her profitability on the deal by 25 percent. She desperately wanted to win the client's business, but she also assumed that the client must be right and that she wasn't "worth" the extra money.

Ironically, what Belinda didn't know was that the client had already decided to award Belinda the contract *before* she agreed to the changes; he was simply "testing the waters" to see if he could negotiate a better deal.

Belinda's experience isn't at all uncommon, says Nancy Long, a former litigator and now mother of two who practices law out of her home. Women frequently find themselves at a disadvantage in the negotiating process and often avoid it altogether by capitulating immediately to the other party's demands. It's a simple matter of self-esteem and knowing one's worth, says Nancy. "Women and men are treated differently from birth. Women are nurturers. They are told they shouldn't be aggressive, and when they *do* decide to take a position, they are seen as bitches." Men, on the other hand, are applauded for being strong and aggressive and maintaining a position. Nancy often negotiates successfully on behalf of her clients and offers the following tips based on her experience:

- *Know your worth.* Don't make the mistake of undervaluing yourself just because you work from home. If you are providing a service, you should set your pricing according to your knowledge, expertise, and experience, all of which has *nothing* to do with your physical location. You can't negotiate if you are unclear about your value.

- *Always use a contract.* A contract formalizes everyone's intentions and enables you to clarify issues at the beginning of the relationship. This is the most important time to negotiate. Most problems arise because nuts-and-bolts issues, such as timing, pricing, and delivery, were not established and agreed upon up front.

- *Think of negotiating as "win-win."* Negotiating doesn't have to be an adversarial process. Think of it more in terms of "give and take." Your ultimate goal is to reach a mutually satisfactory agreement by looking for favorable middle ground.

- *Step back.* Don't be afraid to step back from the negotiating table to give yourself time to think. Don't automatically capitulate because you feel the need to make an immediate decision. If you're negotiating on the phone, tell the person you'll call him back in a few minutes if you feel you need time to think.

- *Take a course and/or find a mentor.* If the concept of negotiating fazes you, attend a seminar or workshop that will give you some guidelines and hands-on experience. If you know of someone in your line of business who regularly negotiates her way to good deals, ask for her advice. And role-play if possible.

- *Get money up front.* In the event that a project has gone wrong and you find yourself negotiating to resolve a conflict, you'll be in a much stronger position if you have already received partial payment. Also, if a client is unwilling to pay a deposit, you may find him unwilling to pay you later.

- *Stand firm.* Although some people negotiate everything on principle just to see how far they can push the envelope, most people simply want the most product or service for the least amount of money. It is your job to convince them that they need your product or service—on the terms you have established.

- *Build in negotiating room.* Build some leeway into your contracts and proposals so that you can afford to give up a little. You'll have room to maneuver during the negotiating process, and your client will feel satisfied that he has won some points, too.

Getting involved in legal wrangles and disagreements can be time consuming and emotionally draining. But you will have some protection if you establish a sound set of business policies and procedures at the outset, and *make sure your customers are aware of them.* Think of it as smart planning—it might take some thought and effort initially, but will save you much *more* time in the long run if you find yourself embroiled in a dispute.

8

Your Business Image

One of the first lessons you probably learned at your mother's knee—and in turn are teaching your own children—is the golden rule: Do unto others as you would have them do unto you.

That rule follows us throughout our life, and it is a rule we never outgrow. We apply it to our family life, our friendships, and if we're smart, our businesses. Every customer, every client everywhere, wants to be treated well, and that includes you as a consumer, too.

If you have ever been treated badly by a business or organization, you probably remember every detail of the incident and will eagerly pass the information on to family and friends. You will no doubt encourage them to boycott the business as a show of support for you. Will they? Maybe not. But they *will* hesitate before using the business, especially if there are other good choices.

A disgruntled client is your business's worst enemy and is capable of doing irreparable harm to your business reputation. Obviously you want to do everything possible to keep your clients happy and pleased with the service you provide so that they will keep coming back to you. How? We call it "the first-class approach." Treat *them* as if they were *you*. You know what you expect from any business you rely on for service. When you call for a pizza delivery, you want it soon, and you want it hot. If it comes any other way, you'll call someone else next time you want pizza. You expect your clothes to come back clean and crisp from the dry cleaners and to be ready for pickup when promised. You know what you want from your favorite store—helpful salespeople, a fair refund policy, quality products, and convenient hours. One unpleasant experience and you will take your business elsewhere.

Your clients will use the same guidelines to assess your business. They will expect fair prices, good service, personalized attention, and a guarantee or refund policy in case they have a problem. If you give them what they want and consistently offer quality service, you can guarantee that each client you work with will act as a walking, talking marketing tool for your business. A little care and concern for each client's satisfaction goes a long, long way in promoting the growth of your enterprise.

Think about the businesses you use most often and why you go back to them time and again; then try this exercise to help you analyze business practices that work. For example, your favorite restaurant: Is it the menu, the atmosphere, the service? Your favorite plumber: Does he show up when he says he will; does he do a good job at a fair price; does he stand behind his work? Your favorite skin-care consultant: Does she offer you good products at a fair price; does she contact you when your favorite product is on sale? Grab a notebook and list any reason that you can think of to explain why you continue to visit, call, or consistently order from these businesses. Then take these methods of customer service and apply them to your own business. If you have one ingredient that creates customer satisfaction, that's good for your business. If you have several ingredients that, combined, can almost guarantee customer satisfaction, then that's *great* for your business.

The Golden Rules of Good Service

Return calls promptly. You know how frustrating it can be to wait several days for a return call from a company when you have made an inquiry. It makes you wonder whether they really want your business! Your customers will feel the same way. If you know you are going to be out of town for more than a day or two, make sure you don't just leave your clients and prospects "hanging." Make it clear in your outgoing message that your office will be closed for a time and let telephone callers know when they can expect a return call. Alternatively (and preferably), check your messages daily and return phone calls from your vacation spot. Don't let calls go unreturned for days at a time and then expect clients to be understanding when you finally get back to them; your credibility is probably beyond saving!

Follow up with your clients. Make it a habit to check back with your clients to make sure they are satisfied with your product or service. Receiving a follow-up call from you will come as a pleasant surprise to your client and differentiate your business from others that don't bother with the "personal touch." Usually the news will be good, but if there is a problem, you'll catch it early and have a chance to fix it.

For example, remember Marilyn, our wreath maker? She put together a lovely custom wreath and delivered it on time to Mrs. Smith, her delighted client. As was her usual business practice, Marilyn followed up with a telephone call a few days later:

MARILYN: Hi, this is Marilyn from Marilyn's Custom Wreaths. How are you, Mrs. Smith?

MRS. SMITH: Oh, hello. Fine, thanks.

MARILYN: I was calling to see how you liked your wreath once you hung it up. Are you pleased with it?

MRS. SMITH: Well, actually, as I started to hang it, the wreath hanger on the back fell off. Several of the flowers came off, too, so I didn't put it up.

MARILYN: Oh, I'm so sorry. I wish you had called to let me know there was a problem.

MRS. SMITH: Well, I thought about calling, but I didn't want to make a fuss. I figured I'd get around to fixing it eventually.

MARILYN: Please let me rectify this right away. I will pick up the wreath tomorrow morning, fix it, and have it back to you with a properly secured hanger tomorrow afternoon. I'll also include a coupon for five dollars off your next purchase to make up for the inconvenience you have experienced. I hope in the future you will contact me immediately if you have any trouble with any of my products. Your satisfaction is very important to me.

If Marilyn hadn't made this follow-up call, she might never have known what had happened; consequently, she wouldn't have had the opportunity to correct it. Her client may not have shared the information with others, but she almost certainly wouldn't recommend Marilyn's business to her friends, either. Instead, because of the prompt attention Marilyn gave her, Mrs. Smith is pleased and impressed and much more likely to remember the fact that her problem was taken care of quickly and efficiently than the specifics of the problem itself.

Express your gratitude. Every client is important to your business and should feel appreciated as such. Receiving a thank-you note from a business you frequent is about as common as a big lottery win! This is an opportunity for you to set your business apart from the competition.

In fact, keep a stock of thank-you notes on hand or have some printed for you. Personalize each note with a brief handwritten message that lets the client know that you value her business and you will work hard to keep it. Do the same for any business or individual who helps you—a referral, help with a project, or an extra discount on something you purchase. In a day and age when everyday consideration for others is uncommon, they will appreciate the gesture. Take the time and do it!

Conducting Yourself Professionally

Look professional in print. Much of your image is what people see. We have discussed the importance of a smart, attractive logo. Make sure that all your printed materials look professional and crisp.

Don't be late. If you schedule a meeting for 3:00 P.M., be there at 2:55! If something crops up unexpectedly, call your client to explain that you will be late and be prepared to reschedule the appointment if necessary. The worst thing you can do is to show up late or not at all. Your business reputation will not survive constant tardiness. If you are habitually late by nature, set your watch a half hour ahead.

Know your weaknesses and limitations. If your client makes a request that you don't think you can fulfill at your usual quality standards, then decline the job, refer it elsewhere, or find someone who can do it for you as a subcontractor.

Be personable. We don't suggest that every client become your best buddy, but take the time to ask how they and their family are doing and acknowledge important events in their lives—a new baby, a new business, birthdays, and special holidays. Not only will clients appreciate your thoughtfulness, but as a marketing ploy, it does keep your business in front of them every time you send a card or other correspondence.

Know when to downplay your role as a mom. These days it is not at all unusual to meet a businesswoman who is wearing many hats. In some cases, it will be positively beneficial to talk up your role as mom and entrepreneur, particularly if your clientele is mainly moms and families. But there are times when clients will not appreciate hearing about your children and how you fit your work in around requests for peanut-butter-and-jelly sandwiches, diaper changes, and story time. You should never try to conduct a telephone conversation with children screaming or playing noisily in the background or interrupt a conversation with your client to talk to your child. Don't take your kids with you to make deliveries or pick up work unless you have been specifically invited to do so (and if you do take them, make sure they behave appropriately). You should also avoid the temptation to share your "war-stories"—even if you are amazed at the hurdles you overcame to get something done! For example, "I can't believe I met your deadline on this project, Mrs. Client, because Johnny jammed Legos into the computer drive and then the baby threw up on the artwork...but I stayed up all night so

I could get it finished in time!" You may think your client will be impressed with your dedication, but she'll just think you run a sloppy operation and will probably take future work elsewhere. The point is, if you are going to talk about being a mom or the importance of your children in your life, make it positive, upbeat, and of benefit to the client to hear.

These are just a few ways you can implement a "first-class approach." You will come up with other ideas yourself. At some time or another, every business experiences unhappy clients, lost orders, billing problems, etc., because no business is perfect. If you project a positive image, your business will thrive even when facing problems. And your customers will respect the way you tackle their problems and resolve these issues.

Congratulations!

You have completed Phase I of this book, and you are well on your way to becoming a home-based business mom! You have established a foundation for your business and in Phase II you will learn how to build upon that strong beginning. Pat yourself on the back, treat yourself to lunch at a favorite restaurant, or simply toast your progress.

And so we take you to Phase II.

Checklist for Phase I

☐ I have read the introduction carefully, completed the income-evaluation work sheet, and concluded that starting a home-based business is the right choice for me.

☐ I have completed the Recipe for Success and have decided to start a business as a _____.

☐ I have decided to purchase a license or franchise _____ (if checked, skip to number 7).

☐ I have decided to start a scratch business.

☐ I have researched my chosen business name in the jurisdiction in which I will be doing business.

☐ I have selected and set up a work space in my home that is convenient, easily accessible, and pleasant.

☐ I have thought about my child-care options and made arrangements with the individuals I will be depending on for help.

☐ I have budgeted for and purchased the electronic items I will need to get started.

☐ I have researched my start-up expenses and decided on a figure that will be sufficient to set up my business and cover my initial marketing expenses.

☐ I know where these funds will be coming from.

☐ I have chosen a bank for my business and have set up an account for my business activities.

☐ I have installed the necessary business software or implemented manual systems to keep track of accounting issues.

☐ I plan to use my existing online connection/get an online connection for:
marketing   selling   networking   resources
creating a business   all the above!   other

☐ I have contacted my local government offices and obtained the required licenses and permits to run a business from my home.

☐ I have contacted my insurance agent and added appropriate insurance policies to cover my business activities and equipment.

☐ I have considered the ramifications of incorporating my business and have decided: to incorporate _____ not to incorporate _____.

☐ I am going to register a trademark now or hold off on registering a trademark because _____ (circle one).

☐ I have established policies and procedures for my business.

☐ I have drawn up a contract to use in my business, or I am contacting an attorney to help me do so (circle one).

Phase II

The Balancing Act

Any mother—let's make that *every* mother—who is trying to run a business while raising a family will tell you that the one thing she could use more than anything else in the world is an extra twenty hours in each day. Wouldn't that be great! She could get a good eight hours of sleep, work about eight hours on her business, run errands, feed the family, clean the house, take a shower that lasted longer than the average sneeze, and *still* have quality time with her children and husband.

Realistically, though—like us—you will struggle to squeeze the demands of your family, domestic responsibilities, and too little sleep into the twenty-four hours you have each day, which at times may seem impossible. But it's not hopeless! The key is to devise a realistic time-management system that is tailored to your own family situation.

The fact is that children, it seems, are programmed at birth to generate surprises that will derail even the most organized of us! This means that on a day that you have an important meeting scheduled with a client, the baby will wake up with an ear infection and a fever of 103 degrees. Or your preschooler will fall off the swing set in the backyard just as you are getting ready to leave and sustain an injury that requires professional attention. Baby-sitters will cancel minutes before you are scheduled to make a delivery or meet with a client. Husbands will arrive late from work on the very evening you are booked to give a lecture on your business. Clients will drop in unexpectedly when your home is in utter chaos, the children are out of sorts, and you still haven't made it to the shower at 2:00 P.M. Our advice? Spend some time on *how you will spend your time.*

The basic premise behind your time-management strategy is to *allow* for the unexpected. Actually schedule "just in case time" into your daily calendar. If you have a meeting set for 2:00 P.M., be dressed and ready to go by 1:00 P.M. This gives you one whole hour to attack any crisis that arises.The following pages will help you plan, organize, and balance your workload. Even on those days when nothing seems to be working, it will help you survive until the next twenty-four hours hits. So read on and discover a whole new meaning to "balance."

9

Setting a Schedule

If you cater to businesses that operate between 9:00 A.M. and 5:00 P.M., it won't do your business much good to set aside evenings for work. On the other hand, if you decide to tutor children after school, you'll have a tough time finding clients if you only operate between 9:00 A.M. and noon. Obviously, you must establish hours that work within the target market you have identified. If clients can't find you when they expect to and they aren't available when you are trying to market to them, your business will never get off the ground.

Designating Business Hours

How do you identify which hours of the day will work best for you? Here are a few questions to ask yourself:

- Do I cater to a specific group? If so, what group?
- At what hours of the day can I most easily access my clients?
- What time(s) of day can I count on help from baby-sitters, my husband, or friends who can watch the children?
- Which hours at home are my worst and least productive?

- Which hours of the day are my best and most productive? Is it early in the morning, before the children wake up? Late at night, after everyone has gone to bed? Or during afternoon nap time?

The answers to these questions should help you determine which hours to designate for your business activities. Allocate time for client contact, marketing, and follow-up; for general office or production work; to do paperwork and accounting; and time you can use for general catch-up.

You may find that you have less time than you had hoped for, but it won't be long before you have figured out how to make the most of every moment!

Let's look at an example. A new mother decides to start a business offering editing and proofreading services from her home. She identifies her target market as printers, graphic designers, and other businesses that most likely keep standard office hours of 9:00 A.M. to 5:00 P.M. She knows that her own personal peak time is in the morning, when her energy level is at its highest and she finds it easiest to focus on her work. Here is how she sets up her work schedule:

6:30–7:30	Wake up, read newspaper, shower, do hair, and put on makeup before baby wakes up.
7:30–8:30	Get baby up. Feed and dress baby. Pack diaper bag. Get dressed.
8:30–9:00	Take baby to sitter.
9:00–11:45	Work on business—client appointments, marketing, telephone calls, etc.
noon	Pick up baby.
12:30–1:30	Have lunch, feed baby, catch up on household chores, put baby down for nap.
1:30–4:00	Work on business.
4:00–5:00	Playtime with baby.
5:00–7:00	Feed baby, prepare dinner, eat with husband.
7:00–7:30	Bathe baby and put him to bed.

7:30–8:00   Clean dishes and pick up toys.

8:00–10:00 Return to office to do paperwork; or use as personal time.

On the days she follows this schedule, she can count on at least five uninterrupted hours to work and even more if she goes back to her office in the evening. She has also still had time with her baby and time to take care of the house.

This is just an example and a guideline; use it to make up a work sheet that will work for you. Obviously, if you have more than one child or a different type of business, you will no doubt break your time down differently.

What If You're Single?

If you are single or divorced, obviously you have a heavier burden than moms who have a loving, supportive spouse by their sides. But it is possible to make a home-based business work as long as the financial pressure isn't too great.

A Personal Glimpse   Cathy McDiarmid is a divorced mom with three boys and runs Born to Love, a mail-order business selling natural baby and mom products, such as cloth diapers, nursing wear and bras, breast pumps, and baby-food grinders. She has always worked with her children around her, in addition to home-schooling her youngest son, Josh. Here's a typical day in her life:

6:30   Get up and check E-mail and spend time online.

9:00   Breakfast with Josh and start home-schooling. We break it up into working two to four pages of work sheets every hour on the hour. Between these times I go down to my office and start filling orders and catalog requests while Josh works on the computer. I have to have the mail out by 1:00 P.M., so I often work through lunch. Once the mail is out, I'll relax with lunch and catch up on any catalogs, new product releases, and anything else that came in the mail that day.

The rest of the day is usually spent printing brochures and catalogs, updating computer files, creating invoices for the next day, etc. Home-schooling ends after the last work sheets are finished at 3:00 P.M. Josh waits for his friends to come home from school so that he can go out to play.

4:00   or thereabouts, it's time to check and answer my E-mail again and get caught up on anything not done so far. In between all the above I am also doing housework, such as cleaning bathrooms, doing laundry, sweeping the floor, plus answering the phone, the door, checking faxes that come in, etc.

6:00   I usually start dinner, wash dishes, clean up the kitchen, and return any long-distance calls I need to make, check in with a friend, or just collapse on the couch while dinner is cooking. Evenings are usually spent folding and collating in front of the TV.

Once a week, we also need to go grocery shopping, and another day we do an errand run of filling the postage meter at the post office, going to the library for tons of books, and picking up necessities at the mall. I also do volunteer work one evening a week at a local healing center.

Cathy spends the weekends working on the computer, updating her literature, preparing newsletters and special mailings, and updating computer files.

The Commitment Combination:
Family and Business

The business line rings at the very moment you are helping your fourth-grader with her math, fixing the kids an afternoon snack, or reading to your toddler. Which one gets your attention, and at what point does one seriously interfere with the other? It's a question mothers with home-based businesses struggle with almost daily.

You have chosen to work at home because you want to be more available to your children than working outside the home would allow. Their well-being is your top priority, and they should know that. But your business must take priority sometimes if it is to survive and bring in the additional income you need to *stay* home-based. The art of balancing the two successfully is an ongoing challenge; you'll find yourself constantly adjusting and fine-tuning to accommodate the needs of both as they enter different stages of growth and development.

The techniques you use to succeed at this balancing act will depend largely on the ages of your children. If you are a new mom, you will have quickly learned that your new baby doesn't give a hoot about anyone else's priorities. When it's time to be fed, changed, or cuddled, you'd better drop whatever else you're doing! Toddlers and preschoolers may be a little easier to handle, for they can be distracted for short periods of time, but generally you won't be able to count on them understanding that Mommy has to do anything that is more important than meeting their needs—instantly!

Children of school age can, and should, learn to wait sometimes. Obviously, you don't want to interrupt your child to take a business call if she is telling you about a problem at school or is upset over a disagreement with her best friend. That's when you let your answering system take the call. On the other hand, if you are *expecting* an important call or visit from a client, tell your child beforehand and assure her that you will be back to continue your conversation as soon as possible.

Here are some rules for maintaining a harmonious balance between your family and your business.

■ *Try getting up earlier than the children.* This will give you some time in your office to get organized for the day ahead. If you work better in the evening, take a block of time after everyone is in bed to return to your office and prepare for the following day.

■ *Don't overdo things if you have recently had a baby.* It's normal to feel overwhelmed and fatigued if your baby is very little, particularly if you are nursing and up frequently during the night. Rest when the baby rests if you need to, but if your energy level is good, by all means put that energy to work. Use nap time as a time to catch up on office chores or as an opportunity to make or return calls with no background noise.

■ *Refer back to our section on child-care options and get help!* Even for a few hours each day. If you have school-age children, schedule your workday around their time at school. If you have toddlers, take our advice and use whatever options might be available to you. If you have difficulty finding quality part-time care during the morning hours, consider hiring a teenage sitter to come in after school and care for the children while you work.

■ *Include the children in your business.* Make them feel appreciated when they help you. There are all sorts of age-appropriate tasks you can find for children: straightening bookshelves, licking envelopes, organizing your office-supply drawer, filing, alphabetizing customer records, folding fliers, and even sorting paper clips. They will soak up any praise you give them for a job well done and feel as if they are part of your success, too. Occasionally reward their efforts with pocket change or an outing to a favorite place.

■ *Set aside a block of time during the day that belongs solely to your children.* Don't schedule any calls or allow yourself to answer the phone or work on your business during this time. If you have to impinge on this special time because of a business crisis, make sure you find time later.

■ *Make the most of the evening meal with your family.* Use this time to catch up on the children's day, share plans, and simply talk "family." You will find that this small act really does reinforce your family bonds. Make sure the TV is turned off during mealtime so that you don't have to compete for your children's attention.

■ *Plan at least one fun outing with your children each week.* The local playground (indoor or outdoor), the library, a trip to the toy store, an ice cream adventure, or your own personal favorite. Make it a date and mark it on your calendar. Try to pick a day at the end of your workweek. It will give everyone something to look forward to; more importantly, it will help motivate your children to cooperate during the week if they know that Friday is treat day.

■ *Know when to stop.* It can be annoying and frustrating to drop what you are doing for what seems to be a minor problem. But from your child's point of view he is grappling with a huge crisis. Our advice? Stop working, give your full attention to your child, and help him solve his problem. These moments reinforce your commitment to your children and reassure them that they are still number one with mom. The business can wait.

■ *Take a weekend off.* Every family needs a period of time together when the focus is on each other. No phones, no meetings, no office work. Almost everyone who works outside the home leaves the office on Friday and returns to work on Monday. You, too, should have time to share with your family, away from your business and guilt-free! Plan for at least one or two of these "family weekends" per month, mark them on your calendar, and stick to the agenda. Don't be tempted to go near your office. You deserve a break, so take it! Your family will appreciate it.

■ *Keep your family involved and interested.* Share important events and achievements in your business with your husband and older children. They will be excited about your progress and proud of your success. Don't forget that this can be an invaluable learning experience for your children. By watching and helping you expand your business, they will see firsthand the importance of the work ethic. They can learn a good deal from a book, but they can learn even more from example.

Will following these guidelines guarantee you a perfect balance between family and work? No. Nothing is a sure thing, and there will be those days when nothing works and everything falls apart and you are not sure who is crying harder—you or your children. We all have days like that. But sticking to these basic guidelines will help you construct a solid framework for managing your time as well as possible.

Keeping Your Cool During Summer Vacation

If you have school-age children, you will probably build your work schedule around the hours they are at school. So what happens during summer vacation? Chaos, potentially! After all, you can't just close your doors for three months every summer! Here are some tips on getting through this somewhat chaotic time:

- *Plan ahead.* Start planning your summer as early as possible. Check into available summer camp programs for your grade-schoolers. Many communities offer half- or full-day recreational programs for a nominal fee during the summer.

- *Be flexible.* Your work schedule during the school year is defined by school hours, bus pickups, and after-school activities. You'll need to be prepared to change your routine during the summer months. Try getting up an hour earlier or going to bed an hour later to buy yourself a bit more time.

- *Go with the flow.* For many businesses, summer is a slow time of year, anyway. You can use this to your advantage by slowing down. Use the time to review your business strategy and marketing techniques and catch up on filing and correspondence. If, however, your business is seasonal and summer is your busiest time, you will need to make arrangements to ensure that you can cope.

- *Put the kids to work!* This is a great time to let the children help you in your business. Draw up a list of regular activities that need to be done and assign them tasks. Let them know that if you get your business work done each day, you will be able to fit in trips to the pool, the zoo, or other places they want to visit.

- *Get creative.*
  - Move your business poolside! Take your laptop computer or files to the pool and work on your business while the children swim.
  - Make arrangements with another home-based mom to "co-op" your businesses through the summer; you'll do her bookkeeping and she'll update your marketing materials.
  - Hire a teen or college student to work part-time taking

calls and working on other aspects of your business. Treat it like an "internship" and the student will get credit for the time she spends with you.

Summertime is hot and humid, and you might have trouble staying focused, but fall is just around the corner. It's not too early to start planning for next year!

10

Time-Saving Tips to Make Life Easier

Unfortunately this book does not come complete with a forty-eight hour day tucked neatly inside for you to use on those days when you're dealing with the "Mother-load," but we have come up with a few ways to stretch the twenty-four hour day that you are guaranteed. Put a few of these into practice and watch your day expand just a little.

Daily Planning

As a home-based business mom, you'll be juggling many roles—business owner, mom, homemaker, and cook—and just the sheer volume of daily tasks vying for your attention can seem overwhelming. You may wonder how you will be able to carve out time for your business in what is an already hectic daily schedule. But you can do it. The key is careful organization and planning.

If you tend to be very organized, anyway, you probably already use some type of time-management system that works well for you.

But for those of us who are less adept at managing our time it may be helpful to consider the following suggestions.

The first step in mastering this challenge is simply training yourself to think ahead and plan your time. And the only tools you need are a "master calendar" and a weekly or daily planner.

The Master Calendar

You probably already have a calendar in your kitchen on which you record all the appointments you make for yourself and your family—well-baby checks, dental visits, school events, and so on. Now you'll need to add your business appointments.

If your existing calendar doesn't have nice big squares to write in multiple entries, buy another one! Don't forget to write in *every* commitment you make—both business and personal. You might want to color-code your entries to more easily identify which is which.

If you find it easier to keep one calendar in the kitchen for personal stuff and a desk calendar to record your business activities, just make sure you cross-reference them every time you make an entry. Your calendar(s) will act as a master planner—a map that outlines your objectives and ensures that you schedule the time to meet them.

Weekly or Daily Planner

Whereas your master calendar gives you a sense of the big picture and shows at a glance everything you have scheduled month by month, you also need a tool to help you plan your time in more detail. That is where your planners come into play. For some, a weekly planner will be enough—an outline for each week that you use to more specifically budget your time day by day. But when you first start your business, you might find it necessary to schedule your days hour by hour until you fall into a pattern that feels comfortable and can be done on autopilot. If you work better when you have all your time accounted for, a daily planner sheet that you work on each evening for the following day will help keep you on track.

Take into account your own personal preferences as you do this.

Everyone will have different circumstances and constraints that shape their own schedules, and some individuals would find it quite depressing to be faced with a totally full daily planner sheet every morning! But having a plan for each day, with items that can be checked off as they are completed, does allow you to see what you have accomplished—especially valuable on the days when it feels as if you didn't get much done at all!

Remember, though, that you need to be realistic when mapping out your time. Don't try to squeeze in too much. You'll just end up frustrated because you didn't get everything done. It's better to allow a little *more* time for each task than you will actually need. This practice makes room for a fussy baby who needs holding and cuddling or a tired toddler who needs to be calmed down before nap time, or for an unplanned visit from a friend or neighbor. If you think you'll need thirty minutes for a task, schedule forty-five minutes instead. By keeping one step ahead of yourself, you may just find a little more personal time in your day.

Set aside fifteen minutes each evening to fill out your daily planner sheet (you can find these sheets at most office-supply stores, or better yet, make up your own on your computer) so that when you wake up in the morning you will already have a head start on your day.

By carefully planning your day, you will begin to see that perhaps twenty-four hours is just enough time to get it all done. And on those occasions when it's not enough, flip the page to find a whole new set of twenty-four hours waiting just for you.

A Personal Glimpse   Lucasvideo Productions owner Lisa Bosak Lucas knows that the only way she can continue to successfully balance her dual roles of mom and business owner is to be "incredibly organized." The Emmy Award–winning producer and mother of two says, "When I wake up in the morning, I have to know exactly what I'm doing that day. On the days that I work, I'll make sure that I have the kids' clothes ready, their lunches packed, and my briefcase organized and ready to go the night before."

Although being organized comes naturally to Lisa, she also recognizes her own limitations. She knows she doesn't have time to "do it all," so she gets help where she needs it. "Cleaning help is a biggie with me. There are plenty of things I'll do without when things get tight, but biweekly cleaning assistance isn't one of them. I don't have the time to keep our house as clean as I like it, and there's nothing worse than cleaning for hours and having the place trashed as soon as the family gets home. Even if you can only afford a once-a-month going over, it's well worth it. I've found it's a great way to keep family peace."

Lisa also does what she can to ensure that both business and home run smoothly—with a minimum of surprises. "I *am* my business, so the upside is, I'm it. I take on what I want and arrange my own schedule. *But* the downside is, I'm it. I have no one to take over the work if I can't do it. So to minimize the unexpected, I try to stay healthy, with reasonably good food and moderate exercise, and I try to keep my kids healthy, too. I make them wash their hands the minute they walk in the door from preschool or day care, they get a children's vitamin each day, we don't share utensils or glasses—things like that."

Lisa tries to plan her work around the three days her four-year-old daughter attends preschool and her two-year-old son is in family day care. But that's not always easy in Lisa's line of work; as a freelance producer she has to work around clients' needs and production schedules that don't always conform to *her* timetable. While she is able to do all the setup for production projects in her home office, there are days that she has to go out on location to film, and much of the postproduction work requires specialized equipment that she doesn't have at home. Since she is always working with some kind of deadline, Lisa counts on additional baby-sitting backup or help from husband Dave when necessary. Fortunately, his job as anchor for a local news station gives him a reasonable amount of flexibility, and his stable schedule offsets Lisa's more erratic one.

In fact, the family time the Lucases enjoy is extremely important to them. Lisa estimates that they have at least two to three extra hours each day because she works at home, and on most days her husband's work schedule gets him home by 3:00 P.M. "Dave could be making twice what he does now, and I could be in an executive position at a station somewhere, but I don't need the extra money right now. I need a father and a husband."

Lisa acknowledges that one of the most difficult aspects of running a business is the inconsistency. "People think it's a perfect world, but I never know what I'm going to be doing from day to day. I find the inconsistency hard. When it rains it pours, and then I panic when things get slow." Although she can't always control the business ups and downs, Lisa does try to counterbalance the situation by maintaining consistency in areas she *can* control. "Even if I don't have to leave the house for a particular project, I get up about the same time, shower, and dress. I try to keep my kids on a consistent timetable as well—drop them off at day care or preschool and pick them up at the same time each day they're there. It's okay if *my* work schedule changes daily, but I don't ever want my kids to feel they're being shuffled around."

Dinner Shortcuts

Ask a roomful of moms to name their least favorite daily household chore and probably at least half will reply "thinking about what's for dinner." It's happened to all of us. You've been busy all day, and at 4:30 P.M. you realize that you have nothing planned for dinner. You throw open the fridge door looking for inspiration, but all you see is milk, unappetizing leftovers, and condiments. You either make a mad rush to the supermarket (at the absolute worst time of day) or settle for take-out-food—again!

We all spend a great deal of time thinking about meals, shopping for and preparing food, and cleaning up afterward. But you can streamline the process a little and make your life easier.

Plan your meals in advance. The few minutes it takes to plan your meals for the upcoming week or month will more than repay you in time saved later on. A good time to do your meal planning is Sunday, when the daily newspapers are positively bursting with coupons and you can plan your meals around the specials at your local store. The fewer trips you make to the grocery store, the better. You will save yourself time and spend less money. Try to be as thorough as possible when making your major grocery-shopping trip. You will probably need to buy staples, like bread and milk, later in the week, but that shouldn't take long. Here are some ideas for getting the most out of your freezer:

Cook several meals and freeze them. Allocate one or two weekend days a month to do much of your cooking. It will be easier for you if your husband is home to help with the children, and you may even enjoy your time spent creating and cooking! If you don't have a stand-alone freezer, now is the time to make the investment. A fully-stocked freezer can be a busy mom's best friend.

Double up your recipes. If you're going to be cooking, anyway, it won't take much more time to whip up a double batch so that you'll have more to stockpile. Foods that freeze well include:

- *Meat dishes*—stews, casseroles, meat loaf, chili, spaghetti sauce, sloppy joes. (*Note:* For a lower-fat alternative, use ground turkey in place of all or part of the ground beef. It will save you fat and calories, and no one will notice any difference in taste!)

- *Chicken*—baked chicken, curry, cutlets, parmigiana. Cooked chicken leftovers can be frozen and used in chicken salad, chicken soup, etc.

- *Soup*—homemade soup is delicious and nutritious and, accompanied by bread and a salad, can make a meal in itself.

Preprepare foods whenever possible.

- Shape hamburger into patties before you freeze them; you can put them right on the grill or broiler from the freezer.

- Brown ground meat for tacos or spaghetti sauce, drain, cool, and freeze. All you have to do is add your seasonings and sauce and heat for a quick and easy dinner.

- Separate chicken breasts and freeze them individually so that you'll be able to take out what you need without defrosting a whole package. Stock up while they are on sale, put them on a wax paper–

lined cookie sheet, and freeze overnight. (Make sure they aren't touching each other.) The next day you'll be able to pick them up and pop them in a freezer bag.

■ If you're chopping onions or peppers for a recipe, chop up twice or three times as much as you need and freeze the extra—great when you need chopped veggies in a hurry for sauces or homemade pizzas.

■ Buy cheese in bulk, grate it, and freeze it. Saves time when making pizza, grilled-cheese sandwiches, omelets, etc.

■ Make up large batches of pancake, muffin, or other dry baking mixes so that all you have to do is add the liquid ingredients and cook. You can store them in the freezer or any cool, dry place.

Chop a week's worth of vegetables and salad. Carrots, celery, radishes, and broccoli will all stay fresh and crunchy when placed in water, stored in a sealed bowl, and refrigerated. They make great between-meal snacks and are much healthier than reaching for the cookie jar. Lettuce can be washed, dried, wrapped in damp paper towels, and put in a zipper bag for quick and easy salads all week. Also, if you are planning on a stir-fry meal during the week, chop the vegetables and store them in zipper bags; this will cut your prep time in half. And the chopped vegetables will take up less room in your refrigerator.

Other Household Hints

Streamline the laundry. Establish two or three washdays each week, including one weekend day when there are extra hands around to help. Resist the temptation to do laundry on your "off" days. Let the older members of the family know that if they need something laundered on a nonwashday, they will need to do it themselves. If the sight of laundry piled high disturbs you, store it in a hamper or closet until washday. Give older children their own baskets and tell them they are responsible for folding their own clothes and putting them away.

Plan your wardrobe. Separate your business clothes and hang them in a different area of your closet so that they are easy to find. If you need to get dressed for an early-morning business meeting, lay out the clothes you plan to wear the night before, along with any accessories. This will save you time in the morning, when you would otherwise be poring through your closet wondering what to wear. Do the same for the children or have them do it themselves if they are old enough.

Make kids' lunches in batches. Prepare and freeze several sandwiches over the weekend, then simply pack the sandwiches in their lunch bags in the morning. By lunchtime the sandwiches will have thawed nicely. This works for you, too. You won't have to stop work to think about and prepare lunch. There'll be no preparation or cleanup time—a real timesaver all around. (Warning: Do not try this with peanut butter and jelly! That is best prepared on the day you wish to serve it.)

Delegate! It's good for your older children to know that running an efficient household is a team effort. Make a chart and assign duties to each individual capable of helping with household chores. Even children as young as five can be given jobs that will help them feel included and teach them about teamwork. Straightening shoes in closets, feeding and brushing the pet, helping to make the bed— even the tiniest hands are capable of completing these tasks. As your children get older, they can take on cleaning bathrooms, doing laundry, dusting, vacuuming, and mowing the lawn. Rotate the assignments from week to week so that each family member learns how to do each household chore well.

Combine errands whenever possible. Make the most of your flexible schedule and choose a weekday to do the bulk of them. Make lists of errands you need to run and categorize them according to their geographic location. Then, for each trip you make, start with the closest place you need to go and work your way out or start with the farthest and work your way back home. Avoid hopscotching all over town; you'll just waste time and gas.

Buy in bulk. Do your pens and pencils always walk? Do you go through legal pads quickly? Do you use a lot of paper? Buy in bulk. There are dozens of office-supply stores and warehouse stores that allow you to buy in bulk, so take advantage of the savings in time and money. (Some warehouse-type stores charge an annual fee. Don't forget to deduct it!)

Safeguard your keys. Babies and toddlers love keys. They're shiny, they jangle, and they fit so perfectly into those little hands! Imagine you're all dressed up, mentally prepared and ready to meet a new client. There's just one problem: You can't find your car keys. If you have toddlers, you can bet your life savings that they will one day take and hide your keys and you may never find them again! (Both of us have at some time lost an entire set of keys that never resurfaced!) Have duplicate keys made up and put them in a safe place. A good way to keep keys safe is to have a high peg or nail where you *always* hang them upon entering the house.

Shop smart. One of the advantages of being home-based and self-employed is that you can set your own hours; you're not tied to a desk for eight hours every day. This means that you can do most of your shopping during the week at off-peak times—a real boon during holiday seasons. You can avoid that awful wait in traffic and to park, and purchase, and then another wait in traffic to get home! In fact, train yourself to spot bargains throughout the year, purchase them, and put them away. The gift-buying season may seem far off in the spring and summer months, but it will be here way before you know it. Consider budgeting so that you can take advantage of postholiday sales. You can find some real bargains the day after Christmas and even more in January.

Be phone-smart. It's becoming increasingly rare to reach a live operator when you place a call. Instead, you are likely to be confronted with an automated system that tells you to make a selection from a lengthy phone menu. Most times you can bypass the menu and reach the operator by simply touching the zero. He or she will usually get you to the right place much more efficiently.

Be firm with telemarketers. They are trained to keep you on the line until you say "uncle." Simply tell them, "No, thank you," and hang up. If you find saying no difficult, interrupt them and tell them it's not convenient now; would they please call back some other time.

Consider getting a caller ID system or setting up special identifying telephone rings for family and friends so that you know who is calling before you pick up the phone. There's nothing more annoying than interrupting your train of thought to answer the phone, only to find it's a call you would rather not have taken.

Stay on top of your mail. Set up two baskets—one for personal and one for business mail—and sort it as soon as it arrives. Then spend one evening a week going through the personal mail and one evening on the business stuff. Be ruthless! Throw out anything you don't need, and if you do need it, put it in an action file or file it with your other papers. Nothing is quite as cleansing as seeing the bottom of those baskets after reading mail, paying bills, and filing statements.

Use the radio for company. It's easy to get used to having the TV on for company while you work around the house—either for personal or business reasons. But the visual images can be distracting, and you may find yourself wasting valuable work time. A better alternative is to turn on the radio or the stereo. It will still keep you company but won't require your full attention.

There are so many ways to steal minutes back from your day and still accomplish a great deal. These are just a few ways that can work for you. You will come up with your own strategies as you become adept at managing and organizing the hours that make up your day.

A Personal Glimpse   Nanci Slagle and Tara Wohlenhaus are two busy moms, with seven kids between them, who know all about the problems mothers have with that daily chore from hell known as dinner. In fact, their business, *30 Day Gourmet,* grew out of their own homespun efforts to simplify and organize meal preparation.

In 1993, the friends attended a workshop on cooking and freezing meals in bulk. Nanci and Tara decided to implement a joint monthly cookfest, and after "stumbling around for the first couple of years," they began to record their activities, recipes, and shopping lists to

---

Time Management Tips

- Use lists to stay organized.
- Work from your "to do" list and cross items off as you do them.
- Learn to say no to teachers, neighbors, friends, and relatives if you don't have time to do what they are asking.
- Use fax and E-mail whenever possible; they're more efficient than lengthy phone calls.
- Set deadlines for yourself.
- Keep a time log for a while and track how you use your time.
- Identify your peak energy periods during the day and do the most important tasks then.
- Use technology to save time. The financial investment will pay off in increased productivity.
- Delegate tasks to other family members whenever possible.
- Organize your space; have a place for everything and keep everything in its place. You'll save hours by being able to access things instantly.

---

help them get better organized. These detailed notes became the basis for the manual they developed and now sell. The *30 Day Gourmet* began as "the determined attempt of two busy, frustrated women to feed their families well." Its primary purpose is to help mothers prepare a month's worth of main dish entrées for the freezer in one day. The manual includes sixty freezable recipes, along with information on organizing and streamlining the process of preparing nutritious, economical home-cooked meals.

The company has grown in leaps and bounds, helped by television exposure and an active website that has boosted sales to the tune of $250,000 in their most recent year of operation. The two partners complement each other well. Tara explains, "I am the cooking half of this partnership. When Nanci and I decided to cook together the first time, we agreed to each bring to our planning session ten favorite recipes, then weed out the ones we knew the other family wouldn't eat. I showed up with about thirty of my favorite little recipe cards (I liked them all and couldn't decide!), and Nanci showed up with a couple of recipes and lots of ideas." Nanci admits that she hates to cook, but her input and business savvy play an equally vital role in the partnership, says Tara. "Nanci is a real hustler. She is really good at grabbing up any free publicity opportunities—newspapers, radio, and television."

Although both women keep an office at home and do much of their work there, they recently moved their main operation out of Nanci's basement and now have a "full-fledged office complete with a full-time office manager and part-time employees. We mainly hire our friends—moms who want to make a few dollars and work the number of hours that fits into their schedules."

The trials and tribulations of entrepreneurship have been rewarding—and educational—as Tara and Nanci have learned to juggle the demands of family and business, along with a busy schedule of television and radio appearances all over the country! Their top tips for staying on top of things:

- Teach your children to never interrupt a telephone conversation unless someone is bleeding or unconscious! Screaming and shrieking fall under the same rules. This is very important for those of us who do not have an office that can be closed off from the rest of the world.

- Be versatile and keep your options open. You might need to change a method or a focus in an instant when necessary. Don't be afraid to change or take chances!

- Don't try to do everything by yourself. It's impossible to be accountants, advertisers, secretaries, shipping clerks, graphic artists, etc., all at the same time. Networking to find people who are competent and compatible with your business style is important.

There's no doubt that getting and staying organized will help you stay on track as you perform the daily family-business shuffle. Take the ideas and suggestions included here, adapt them to suit your own personal situation and then throw in some ideas of your own. Take stock of where you are every so often—review the techniques and strategies you have been using to stay on top of your busy schedule and make any necessary adjustments. You and your family will benefit, and so will your business.

11

Getting Motivated

It's so easy to be filled with energy and enthusiasm over something brand-new, whether it's a home, a car, a job, or a business. The excitement of a fresh challenge keeps you motivated and focused at first, but as time goes on and the novelty wears off, you may feel your energy level begin to wane.

In most aspects of our lives, sooner or later we'll find it a struggle to stay on top of things and maintain the interest with which we started. It will be no different with your business. It takes your time, effort, and energy. It takes you away from your family and friends and at times can rob you of much-needed rest. And initially the meager income it produces won't seem to justify the time you spend on it. On days when things go wrong, a client yells at you, or you're tired from taking care of sick children and can't see your desk for paper, you may be tempted to call it quits. Of course, since it's your business, the decision is entirely yours to make! But you've come too far to let your business just fade away. Although it can be hard to get charged up again, remember that this is a normal, cyclical feeling that we all experience at one time or another, and yes, you can get the fervor back!

First of all, you need to figure out what caused you to lose interest and become demotivated. You need to identify the problem before you can hope to address it and eliminate it. For example, if you find that you are tired and lethargic because you are staying up late to do paperwork, you should rethink your schedule. Maybe a switch to early mornings would suit you better.

Perhaps you are feeling isolated and alone because you don't have enough interaction with other adults. The solution could be as simple as joining a networking group and getting out to meetings once or twice a month. Possibly you have realized that you absolutely despise marketing and keep making excuses to avoid it. You could hire someone else to do some marketing for you, or better yet, barter with another mom who needs help with something *you* are good at. The point is, there is a way to resolve most of the problems you might run into—once you have pinpointed the cause.

One of the most common reasons for feeling discouraged is that, despite your best efforts, the volume of business simply isn't what you had hoped for. Some creative marketing may be in order to get things moving. After all, nothing is quite as energizing as a surge in business, accompanied, of course, by a corresponding increase in your bottom line! (See Phase III for our suggestions on marketing.)

Although owning your own home-based business can be fun and exciting, it can also be exhausting and taxing on your family. Include them in the troubleshooting when you're trying to work your way out of a slump. After all, they are part of your team.

What follows in this section should help to keep you motivated and excited about your business. When you feel particularly dis-heartened and need help to get back on track, read through it again. The ideas and suggestions will help you keep a strong and healthy focus on your business; in turn, your business will stay healthy and strong.

A Personal Glimpse   Cheryl Demas was employed full-time as a computer programmer when she found out that her seven-year-old daughter, Nicki, was diabetic. Three days later, she gave birth to Dani. "It was an event-filled week that led to a life-altering decision: I would stay at home full-time with our children."

Cheryl found her business niche shortly afterward designing websites. As her business grew and she realized how many other moms were looking for an alternative to the traditional options of full-time employment or full-time mothering, she founded a news-letter and online magazine for work-at-home moms—WAHM.com. This spin-off from her original business idea has been so successful that Cheryl now devotes most of her time to maintaining the website, which typically receives more than one hundred thousand visits each month and continues to grow.

Staying motivated for Cheryl is a "personal affair":

"My husband and family keep me motivated. I also see how proud my ten-year-old is of my business. We've had some exposure in national magazines, so it's been really neat for Nicki to see her picture and drawings (she does the illustrations for WAHM.com) in the press. I also love what I'm doing. Working from home has been such a great experience for me and my family that I want to help other women do the same thing. When I hear success stories from other moms who are able to stay home with their kids, I have renewed energy to keep going. Even my three-year-old recognizes my website, and when she sees it printed out, she says, "There's your web page, Mommy.""

Cheryl sums it up as follows: "I love being home for my family, not dealing with the daily stress of day care, etc. I also love the interaction with other adults and feeling of accomplishment I get from earning money from my own business. It has helped my self-esteem, and I'm doing what I really love to do."

Rewarding Yourself

Companies worldwide, operating in all languages, know that the key to keeping employees successful and productive is the same in any language–motivation. Companies large and small use all kinds of methods to increase production and at the same time keep employees happy. They call these methods incentives.

An incentive is simply a reward for effort—a prize, a pot of gold at the end of the rainbow. It is a way to help someone see a project through, finish a task, reach a goal. Monetary rewards, vacation packages, gift certificates, and prizes are all used by big business to give employees something to work toward. You, too, can use incentives to help motivate the one and only employee of your company—you.

Of course, the type and size of your incentives will not be on quite the same scale! But you will be able to treat yourself to a little something when you've made progress. Make a list of incentives that will get you going and assign goals you must reach to earn them. Here are a few examples to start you off:

■ Hold off a little longer on purchasing that print you've been eyeing or the piece of furniture you would love to add to the nursery and put it on your incentive list.

■ Upgrade your computer system. When you receive a nice fat check from a project you've completed, spend some of the money on a new software package you've been dying to try or add some additional memory to your computer. Your improved functionality will get you excited again, plus any upgrade you make is an investment in your business, allowing you to offer a better service to your clients.

■ On a personal note, choose an incentive that makes the nonworking side of you happy. Join a health club, or buy a new piece of exercise equipment or a new outfit.

■ Take your husband out to dinner at a special restaurant you've been wanting to try. Dress up and make it a special celebration of your progress.

■ Tuck money away for a special vacation or weekend trip. If you can, have a grandparent take the kids and make it a romantic getaway for you and your husband.

■ Pamper yourself! You're working hard; you deserve it! Treat yourself to a manicure, a new haircut or facial, or a luxurious massage at your favorite salon.

■ Award yourself a "mental-health day" in the middle of the week. Arrange for someone to watch the children and just take off in any direction that suits your fancy. You will come back replenished from the time you spent alone. Take yourself to lunch, or if the weather is good, pack a picnic and your favorite magazine and head to the nearest park.

■ Do something special to your home. Replace the worn, old carpet in the family room, buy new stools for the kitchen counter, or *really* splurge and redecorate an entire room.

■ Hire a cleaning crew to clean your home from top to bottom. It can be overwhelming to run a business and still have the responsibility of household chores. Even if you can't afford a cleaning service on a regular basis, at least treat yourself once in a while.

■ Reorganize your office. Sometimes the clutter gets out of hand, and just walking into your messy office is enough to depress you! Set aside a day to go through it from top to bottom. Throw out anything you don't need and file the rest. It'll work wonders for your frame of mind.

■ Invest in a hobby. Sign up for that pottery class you've been longing to try, or the dance lessons or cooking class. Admittedly, it will be something else to fit into your schedule, but the enjoyment you get from it will justify the extra shuffling.

These are just suggestions. You may feel that some of them wouldn't particularly motivate you personally. Draw up your own list of incentives and organize it by size or affordability, then devise some system of awarding them to yourself. Many of the larger incentives may be out of reach for some time, so give yourself little boosts along the way that will keep you motivated to reach for the "big" rewards. Just remember, every milestone you reach means your business is growing.

We realize that the main reason you are working at home is to add to the family income, and we aren't suggesting that you frivolously

Success Strategies for Moms

- Be realistic. Your home-based business will probably take more time and money than you originally anticipated, so bear that in mind as you plan your business venture.
- Do something you enjoy. It will make those late-night marathons more palatable!
- Take yourself seriously as a businessperson. If you don't, you can't expect others to.
- Surround yourself with positive people who will support your efforts and boost your confidence.
- Be flexible. If your first idea doesn't seem to be working too well, try some minor modifications. Sometimes just a few changes can make all the difference.
- Be prepared for a period when your business isn't making much money. Most new businesses take time to get established before generating significant income.
- Hook up with a mentor or business counselor, if possible, and believe the advice she gives you. She's been where you are and is probably right!
- Discuss your ideas with your spouse. His support could make or break your business venture.
- Invest in some small-business courses or seminars. Many organizations and community colleges offer excellent, bargain-priced courses on basic tax and accounting, business law, marketing, and other essential activities.
- Be bold in your vision and allow yourself to dream.

spend money that has been budgeted for monthly expenses. Nevertheless, with some careful planning you should be able to squeeze out a little to put into building your incentive fund.

Above all, remember that you need to replenish yourself every so often or you will run the risk of burnout. It can be hard to stop and smell the roses, particularly when you are anxious to get your business off the ground, but taking care of yourself along the way will more than compensate for any time "lost" in the process.

Before you can dream up incentives, though, you have to have a goal in mind. Our next section will take you through the process of setting realistic goals and, using your incentives system, reaching them.

Setting Goals and Reaching Them

Every New Year's Eve millions of Americans make a list of resolutions—their goals for the coming year. On most of those lists the same few items crop up time after time—lose weight, exercise more, save money, do better at work, be nicer to the family. In fact, the lists could almost be called generic because so many of the same goals appear on so many different lists. Why don't more people achieve their goals? If everyone did, we'd be the only country in the world where most of the population was svelte, toned, athletic, successful, friendly, and family-oriented!

Unfortunately, few are able to stick with their resolutions long enough to benefit from the results—mainly because people are impatient and unrealistic about how long it will take to reach a goal. Therefore, at some point during the early part of January the list gets tucked in a drawer or tossed in the trash and it is back to life as usual.

For you, successfully growing your business will depend, in part, on your ability to set short-term, realistic, attainable goals. Anything else will just end up discouraging you because it is all too hard to achieve.

Let's look at an example of two moms who start the same type of business—a freelance secretarial service. Mom A decides that she would like to find at least two clients during her first month in business and establishes that as her goal. Mom B, however, wants quick results and will only be satisfied if she signs up at least one new client each week—in other words, four in a month.

They both forge ahead with their marketing efforts, contacting potential clients and following up on leads. The calls pay off, and by the end of her second week our first mom has signed up her first client. Feeling satisfied that her marketing formula is working, she continues the following week, but instead of obtaining one more client to meet her goal, she actually exceeds it when she signs up two more! She is thrilled and energized by her success.

Now, let's check in with Mom B. She also signed up three new clients during her first month in business, but unlike her counterpart, she felt disappointed in herself and started to think that maybe she had made a mistake in going into business in the first place. Even though she had done just as well as her competitor, she could not see past the fact that she had failed to reach her goal and so felt demoralized.

What we see from this is that goals should be taken seriously. Setting a goal creates a mind-set and an expectation about our ability to meet it. If it was unrealistic to begin with, the risk of failure is that much greater. A realistic goal creates a challenge, but not an unbeatable one. We teach our children that they can't run before they can walk, and the same principle applies to any learning endeavor. For us, taking those first baby steps helps us learn about our business and what we can expect from it. It helps us learn and refine our marketing techniques and identify which ones are most effective. Small business, small goals—set one at a time *realistically*—that's the key. Once you have reached your objective, set a new, more ambitious goal for yourself. As you meet and master each new challenge, you will begin to see a pattern of success.

Here are a few tips to remember on setting goals:

■ The moment you reach a goal, reward yourself and set a new one. This practice will keep your business alive and growing simply because you are putting time and energy into it as you strive to meet each goal.

■ Each time you reach a major milestone or overcome a particularly difficult hurdle, your inclination will be to look around the room for someone to share it with—only to find yourself alone! Ring

---

The Goal Jar

If you have trouble deciding on a goal or you have so many in mind that it's difficult to know which one to concentrate on first, try putting together a "goal jar." Jot down five or six objectives on individual pieces of paper and put them in the jar. These objectives could range from "clear out the mail basket" to "bring on two new clients." Choose one piece of paper and focus on that particular goal until you've reached it.

---

your own bell! Celebrate your success by calling friends and family and sharing the news. The "pat on the back" will feel good!

- Set realistic goals! We discussed this earlier but can't stress it enough. If you set your goals too high, you will inevitably be disappointed in your progress.
- If you have difficulty reaching a particular goal, grab some paper and write down the things that are standing in your way. Sometimes seeing a problem on paper puts it in concrete terms, allowing you to dissect it piece by piece until you have spotted the problem. Once you know what the problem is, you can work on resolving it.
- Don't overwork yourself. You can't keep up an unrealistic pace for very long. Sooner or later you'll burn out. Find a comfortable pace that allows you to work, spend time with your family, grow your business, and still feel fulfilled in your personal life. Once you ease yourself into that pace, stick with it!

Becoming an Expert on Your Trade

It may not be our favorite way of spending time, but most of us realize that to become really good at what we do, we must constantly be ready to learn, research, and study. When you were pregnant with your first child, chances are you got several books from the library and read up on what to expect in each trimester. You probably checked your progress regularly and learned breathing techniques in preparation for the birth. You doubtless have a minilibrary of books on child rearing that you can consult to make sure that baby is on track in his or her development. You're becoming quite an expert on motherhood and child care!

You will want to approach your business in the same way. You'll need to learn about your trade and your market, research new developments and discoveries, and study business concepts that will help your business grow and perform to expectations. There is certainly no shortage of learning materials available to help you become an expert on your trade.

Periodicals, Magazines, Newsletters

Almost every trade is covered by one or more industry-specific publications designed to keep subscribers abreast of new trends and changes. If you're not sure how to find them, check out one or two how-to books on your line of business from the local library. Most books will include a resource section at the end in which are listed relevant periodicals, magazines, and newsletters. Write or call for sample copies first. That way you can evaluate how helpful each publication would be to your business before committing yourself to a full subscription. Limit yourself to one or two subscriptions or you'll find yourself inundated with material you don't have time to read. And don't forget that any business-related subscriptions will be tax-deductible.

When your reading material arrives, scan the table of contents for information that you need now and mark it with a little flag. Stash the flagged articles in your diaper bag and catch up on your reading while you wait for an older child to finish a dance lesson or soccer practice. Clip and file articles that you want to keep for future reference and anything else that you think will be helpful to you at some point. Recycle the rest! It's amazing how quickly those slim publications stack up to become an intimidating pile, so it's important to take what you need and discard the rest.

Books

It may seem obvious, but check out at least a couple of books from the library and, if you find them especially helpful, consider buying your own copy so that you can highlight important sections with a marker. Read books on any aspect of your business that you're unsure about, including marketing, accounting, business planning, etc.

On a regular basis, check with the local library for pertinent new books that are on order. Then ask to be called when the book arrives so that you can view it right away. You don't want to wait weeks and weeks to get your hands on it once it is published.

Online Resources

This is probably the most comprehensive source of information on just about any topic you can think of! Not only that, but you can link up with other business moms across the country and share their expertise, too. If you are already online, you know how vast the pool of information available to you is and how hard it can sometimes be to limit your searches to only the relevant stuff. If you decide to surf through occasionally to see what new information is available, try not to get too sidetracked. Get the information you came for and then, if time allows, go into other areas just for fun.

Mentors

Some nonprofit organizations run "mentor" programs where inexperienced businesswomen are hooked up with established business owners who provide help and advice on running the business. If there is a program like this in your area, take advantage of it. There's no better teacher than experience.

Courses and Seminars

Many local community colleges offer business courses that would be of benefit to you. If you have no previous business experience, give serious thought to taking a couple of classes on starting and running a business. If they offer courses specifically on the type of business you have started, take those, too. You won't regret it.

Being well-read will give you an edge over your competition and confidence in your ability to run a successful business. Staying informed on the latest trends and products in your line of work is an important part of providing all you can to your clients and keeping them happy. Moreover, keeping abreast of new and unique methods of marketing, incentives, and other ways to expand your client base will help keep your business alive and kicking. So take the time and become an expert!

A Personal Glimpse   Ann Smith went "back to school" when her company, Ann Smith Communications, Inc., was three years old and recently incorporated. Ann, a media planner and communications consultant, actually grew up in a family business, which gave her a fundamental understanding and knowledge about what was involved. Nevertheless, she felt she needed the validation that a business course would provide and signed up for a twenty-seven-class course offered by a local women's business organization. The course was geared to women who had already been successful in business but recognized the value of additional education as they sought to expand their businesses to another level.

Ann found that the course benefited her in more ways than one: "I felt like I needed the course to confirm that I was doing things right. Working alone at home, it's hard to get feedback on whether you're doing something the right way, and I've always felt that if I don't know something, I should go to school for it. Doing the course boosted my confidence because it showed me that I knew more than I thought! And I also met other women like me who were home-based. We became a support group for each other, and I found myself benefiting from their input; it stimulated all our creative juices. The other advantage was that we were able to use our own businesses almost like a "class project," so the course allowed us to combine practical experience with structured learning in a classroom setting. It gave me whatever I could have wanted from an MBA without actually doing it!"

After taking the course, Ann's next year in business was her best ever, and she credits the course with giving her the confidence to handle the surge in growth. She and the rest of her classmates still meet regularly to network and mentor each other.

12

The Art of Networking

Networking has become a popular buzzword, a concept that is associated with success and achievement. Just what is "networking," anyway? Actually, it's a very natural process. We are all born with the instinct to associate and communicate, to create bonds with those around us who share a common interest. That, at its most basic level, is networking.

You may be surprised to hear that you've been networking without realizing it! How do we know *you* have been networking? Because you're a mom! You network when you go to the playground with your kids and share your daily experiences with the other moms there—everything from dealing with temper tantrums to which diaper performs best. You exchange information, trade tips, and sometimes you come away with new ideas that will make your job a little easier.

You network when you circulate and mingle at a party or other social event, chatting as you go. Sometimes you learn a little, and sometimes you learn a lot. At other times you are the one supplying valuable information. Still, it's networking.

You network anytime you hand out your business card or post it on a bulletin board. You network anytime you appear at a function, whether it relates to your business or not. You network anytime you discuss your business and what it can offer to another individual or group. You are creating an avenue for people to reach you, a line of communication that could benefit both parties, and *that is networking!*

Where, When, and How to Network

Where? Everywhere! When? All the time! How? Confidently and positively! Consider every place you go and every individual you meet a networking opportunity—a chance to talk about your business and make contacts that will lead to new business. Sometimes the contacts you make aren't likely to need your services, but *they* may have contacts who do.

For example, the young, unmarried corporate fast-tracker you meet at a luncheon probably isn't too interested in your nursery-design service, but her sister, who is six months' pregnant with her first child, just might be. Therefore, establishing contact with the young executive could be very worthwhile.

The owner of the local deli makes great sandwiches, but why would he be interested in what you have to offer? You own a desktop publishing business, and he needs his menu redesigned; that's why.

The point is, you never know when talking to others about your business might benefit you. And often you won't see results immediately. It may take several weeks or even months for your contact to develop into a client. For example, when we (Caroline and Tanya) met several years ago through networking, we never realized that our contact might bring us to the point of sharing ideas in a book. Although we continued to stay in touch on and off over the years, it wasn't until eight years after our initial meeting that our contact turned into something more than a casual friendship and we formed our writing partnership. Good things come to those who wait? We think so!

Generally you can find impromptu networking opportunities

everywhere you go—the local library, the playground, McDonald's, the doctor's office, the hair salon. Anytime a conversation leads up to how you spend your days becomes an opportunity to talk about your business and possibly gain a contact.

Generally you'll make the most worthwhile contacts in more formal networking environments, and if you take our advice, you will probably join at least one or two organizations whose only purpose is to facilitate networking among its members. Unlike the casual contacts you make when you're out and about, these functions give you an opportunity to go prepared and make the most of the situation. Remember, through networking, you can meet hundreds of people, and of those hundreds of people, many could be contacts and conduits for your business.

It's easy to get lost in the crowd at a busy networking function, and you want to make sure that the contacts you make leave with a strong, positive impression about you and your business. Here are some ways to be remembered in the best possible way:

Smile! Smiles are contagious and generate warmth.

Be creative. If possible, attach something to your business cards that will make them unique and different. For example, punch a hole in the card and tie on a little play ring (you'll find them at most toy stores for pennies) and simply say as you hand out your card, "Take my card, and I'll hope for a ring back very soon!"

Hand out lollipops you have labeled with your company name and phone and the slogan "I'm a Sucker for Your Business!"

If your business is brand-new, try bubble gum or chocolate cigars announcing the birth of your business. Gimmicky? Yes! Expensive? Yes, creative networking is a little more expensive, but it can give you an edge and add a little lighthearted relief to a sometimes boring networking function. That is your ticket to being remembered. The ten dollars that you spend on trinkets that help you stand out may be well worth it.

Don't be a wallflower! Participate in conversations. People are there to learn about each other, and this is your opportunity to let others know about you and what you do!

Remember that networking is a two-way street. It's not appropriate to launch into a lengthy monologue bragging about how wonderful your business is. People will quickly lose interest in what you are saying and write you off as a self-absorbed bore. You must show interest in others and what their businesses offer, too. After all, you never know when that contact may be someone who can help you.

Be confident! Come up with a short, succinct introduction about you and your business and practice it so you have a great opening line. If you're a little unsure of yourself at first, don't worry. It's only natural, and like everything else, practice makes perfect! Make sure you wear something that you feel good in and that your hair and makeup are in good shape.

Be armed and organized. Bring plenty of business cards and/or brochures to hand out—always more than you think you'll need. Scraps of paper are no substitute! Wear a jacket with pockets on both sides. By doing so, you can keep your business cards on one side and put the cards you are given in the other pocket.

Use memory aids. It's hard to remember who was who after you've spent two or three hours meeting new faces and all you have to help you is a bunch of business cards! After a couple of weeks it'll be even harder. As soon as you get home, scribble some notes about the individual on the back of each business card you collected. Make a note of where and when you met and add a simple physical feature that will jog your memory later on. For example:

> 2/21/97 Home-Based Business Network Meeting
> Red dress, dark hair, glasses. Call in 2 wks. to make appt.

If you use a contact-management or database software program on your computer, customize it to your needs and always input new contacts as soon as you can.

Follow up when appropriate. We often make a really good contact, enjoy a lively discussion, make plans to get in touch and meet again, and then lose momentum because neither one followed up! If you hit it off with someone at a networking function and

---

When *Isn't* It Appropriate to Network?

The answer for most businesspeople is probably never. But we know that as moms in business there are times when it simply doesn't make sense to try to network. For example, you are at the supermarket at the tail end of a difficult day and the children are tired and the baby is cranky. You're wearing that old, stained sweatshirt and jeans and don't exactly look your best, and of course that's when you spot a potential client in the produce section whom you've been trying to reach for weeks. Shouldn't you make the most of this chance meeting? Our advice? Skip it! Neither of you will benefit much from a meeting under those circumstances; in fact, you may want to make a hasty exit before she spots you!

---

there's obviously some potential for business, drop a note or follow up with a phone call soon after your initial meeting. This way you will solidify the connection and progress toward your ultimate goal—getting new business.

Networking is more than just a tool for obtaining clients; it offers people who work alone a vital link to others—something taken for granted in a traditional office setting. As owner of a one-woman business, you will no longer have access to peers and colleagues who can advise you when you run into a problem. Nor do you have a supervisor to pat you on the back for a job well done. Now you have to actively seek out and create your own support environment, and participating in networking organizations can help you do that. There are networking groups for almost everything, but to maximize the benefits of joining, pick one or two networking groups and *actively participate*. The more you put in, the more you'll get back. Most groups are run by volunteers. Ask what you can do to help and jump right in. It'll be wonderful experience for you, and you will be reinforcing your role within the organization.

Starting Your Own Networking Group

You understand the importance of networking, and you're anxious to get started. There's just one problem: You've looked high and low in your area, and there isn't a group for you to join. Solution? Start one!

The home-based business industry is growing in leaps and bounds. Many of these home-based entrepreneurs are women who, like you, have left the work force to be home with children and would welcome a group that catered specifically to their needs. An effective networking group can range from a small, informal group that gets together for lunch once or twice a month to a more formal, larger organization that holds regular meetings with programs and speakers.

Caroline cofounded just such a group in 1990—the year after she had started her business. The suggestions that follow are based on her experience.

"I started my business in September 1989. My oldest child was off to kindergarten five mornings a week, the three-and-a-half-year old twins were in preschool three mornings, and luckily my three-month-old baby took good naps! Obviously, most of my 'free' time was spent on developing my business, but I soon found that I really wanted to connect with other moms who had chosen to work this way, too. I felt like something of an anomaly. Neither moms who worked outside of the home nor those who had chosen to stay home with their children full-time seemed to understand some of the special challenges that confronted me as a home-based business mom. I tried attending a few local businesswomen's networking functions but was really turned off when told that talking about one's children was 'unprofessional' and frowned upon and only 'business' conversations were encouraged. I had made a conscious choice to combine work and family by starting a business at home, and there were issues that arose on a daily basis that involved both aspects of my life. I wasn't prepared to segment my life into business versus family at networking functions when my whole identity was wrapped up in *blending* the two areas as much as I could!

"Commiserating with another mom about this lack of support one day, I popped the question, 'Why don't we start our own networking group—specifically for moms who have a home-based business or who want to work from home?' Within a few short months, my cocommiserator, Linda (a human-resources consultant and single mom of two boys) and I had lined up a meeting space (free of charge), printed fliers, and placed a free announcement in the local paper to publicize the fledgling organization. At our first meeting, in November 1990, we welcomed fifteen other like-minded moms, and more moms found their way to each subsequent meeting. It wasn't long before we had established a schedule of monthly meetings, elected officers and a board, created monthly programs, and booked speakers. MATCH—Mothers' Access to Careers at Home—was born and on its way. Our goals? To provide networking, support, education, and advocacy for moms who wanted to work from home.

"We incorporated, obtained official tax exemption as a nonprofit, and added another chapter in a neighboring state. By the time we honored our first Woman of the Year in 1993—a local mom whose home-based business success was netting her close to $1 million a year—our numbers had swelled to almost one hundred.

"And all this was done by moms volunteering their time, running their businesses, *and* taking care of their families at the same time! So much for unprofessional! Our meetings were a delightful blend of hardcore business issues, tempered with humorous tales of children's antics, pregnancy announcements, and advice on juggling home and business. Breast-feeding moms were encouraged to bring their nursing infants rather than miss a meeting, although we drew the line at toddlers—anyone with a child older than fifteen months will understand why! We urged members to use each other's business services whenever possible, and many moms benefited from the friendly, supportive environment of MATCH as they practiced their networking skills and tried out new marketing techniques."

MATCH is still flourishing, although Caroline moved on a few years ago. While there are moms who want to work from home, there will always be a need for organizations like this. Here are some suggestions for starting your own group:

- Team up with another mom if possible so that two of you are doing the start-up work. Organizing a group from scratch can be time-consuming, and you will be fitting this in around all your existing activities.

- Draft a simple statement defining your vision of what the group will be. Don't be wishy-washy or afraid to make decisions. In the early days, it takes someone with specific ideas and plans to establish a strong foundation. As your membership grows, you will want to appoint a board responsible for running the organization.

- Be creative. Don't spend money unless you have to, or better yet, until you are generating some income from membership dues. Call local churches, schools, community centers, and libraries to find space you can use for meetings. You may need to move several times to accommodate your growing membership or to take advantage of a better location, and that's fine. Don't pay to advertise in the local paper. Use the community-announcements section to promote your meetings.

- Make up fliers to post in supermarkets, libraries, office-supply stores, your children's schools, doctor's offices—in fact, anywhere moms are likely to go. Use colorful paper and preferably some graphics that will attract attention. Make sure to include your phone number so that they can call for more information.

- Look for free publicity. Call your local paper or send them a press release. Perhaps they'll do a feature article on your group or at least list it as a resource in any articles they run on home-based business.

- Be professional at all times. Set the tone for your organization and others will follow suit.

- Schedule meeting times that are convenient. Many networking groups meet at the worst possible times for moms—breakfast time! Evening meetings will work much better for moms depending on husbands to be at home with the children.

- Plan your meetings. Don't let the meetings turn into chat

sessions. Structure them so that members know what to expect each time. For example, a typical meeting might look like this:

7:00–7:30	Check in and general networking time.
7:30–7:45	Introduction to the organization, recognition/introduction of visitors and new members. Member news.
7:45–7:50	Introduction of evening's program and speaker.
7:50–8:35	Presentation of program.
8:35–8:45	Question time.
8:45–9:00	Wrap-up and end of meeting.

Make a point of keeping on time and to your schedule. If possible, have printed agendas available, with general information about the group on the back.

■ Don't be afraid to charge for membership—even early on. Appoint a treasurer to take care of funds and to make sure the money is handled correctly. Don't make the fee outrageous in the beginning, but as your membership increases and the services you offer become more valuable, you can justify increasing the annual dues.

■ Treat your volunteers with respect and consideration. Many a volunteer group has gone by the wayside because volunteers couldn't keep up with unrealistic expectations and demands. Your volunteers are already busy women who are giving up their time to help because they believe in what you are doing. Compliment them and make sure they feel appreciated for what they are contributing.

■ Always send a thank-you note to anyone who has helped by speaking at one of your meetings or made a contribution in some other way.

A networking group can be a place to learn, to grow, to feel validated and at home among peers. You will establish business contacts, make personal friends, and find playmates for your children. Your business will grow as a result, and so will you.

Congratulations!

You have completed Phase II of this book and should now have a very good idea of how your business can and will fit into your life. You should be leaving this phase armed with time management tricks, and ways to stay motivated and deal with the isolation that can sometimes accompany working at home.

In Phase III the focus will be on identifying and reaching your target market—a vital part of building a strong and healthy business. Remember, like anything you value, you will need to nurture your business and occasionally pamper it. It will reward you by staying around for a long time. Kind of like having another child. Now, on to Phase III.

Checklist for Phase II

☐ I have created or bought a daily/weekly planner to help me schedule my business into my day.

☐ I have talked to my family and my spouse about my business plans and how it may affect our time together.

☐ I have made a list of shortcuts and timesaving techniques that apply to my personal situation.

☐ I have thought about ways to keep motivated and made a list of the types of incentives that will help me stay on track.

☐ I have researched and found the following networking groups I am considering joining for marketing, contacts, and support:

_____

_____

☐ I haven't found a networking group in my area but plan to start one (date) _____.

☐ I have researched publications, organizations, and resources that could be helpful to me as follows: _____

_____

_____

_____

_____

Phase III

Growing Your Business

You will quickly find that, unlike your children, your business isn't preprogrammed to grow without significant intervention from you! It will require consistent and persistent effort to build a vital, dynamic business from its embryonic form. Growing your business will be challenging, exciting, exhausting, and exhilarating all at the same time, and you'll become very adept at an activity that is critical to your business growth. It's called marketing, and it's everywhere.

It hits you when you don't even realize it. While you are carpooling the kids, you find yourself humming a jingle for a soft drink that you're not even terribly fond of. At the supermarket you grab the cereal that your favorite celebrity eats and buy the shampoo that supermodels say they use. You buy lottery tickets when the ad says the jackpot is ridiculously high, and you take comfort in knowing that your bathroom tissue is soft enough to use on even the tiniest of bottoms. It's all the result of clever marketing, and it's designed to get you to buy a product or use a service.

It might sound harsh, but your ability to market successfully will make or break your business. You can have the best product in town, the fairest price, and the most dependable service, but if no one knows about it, you don't have a business no matter how good you are.

"Marketing" is simply an umbrella term for all the things you do to create and keep enough customers to support and expand your business. This includes advertising, publicity, sales, and other promotional activities. A good, strong marketing plan and a means of setting it in motion is vital to every business—large or small, office-based or home-based. Marketing is a perfect example of action and reaction. You market effectively; people come for your product or service; your business stays strong and healthy. But if you sit back and assume that sooner or later customers will find you, your business will need life support very early on.

Do you need to consult an expert or hire a marketing firm to get you on your way? Probably not; in fact, we are assuming that your limited budget will preclude it. It may all seem a little intimidating at first, especially if you don't have any prior marketing experience to bolster your confidence, but a little research on your part, coupled with the information and tools in this section, should enable you to devise a solid, workable marketing plan. Plan on spending about 30–40 percent of your time on marketing your business; especially at first. That may seem a lot, and you don't want to neglect other important areas, such as your bookkeeping and administrative tasks, but you won't need to worry about those tasks at all if your marketing efforts aren't effective!

In the pages that follow we will introduce you to several marketing techniques. Not all of them will be appropriate for your business. For example, posting fliers on the supermarket bulletin board isn't likely to bring in too many leads for an attorney specializing in patents and copyrights! However, if you run a day-care business in your home or offer gardening or sewing lessons to youngsters, that very same bulletin board will no doubt bring in a very promising response. Keep in mind the kind of business you are running and who it is geared toward as you develop a marketing plan that will work for you.

Have a notebook handy to jot down ideas as you read and study this important section. Go at your own pace and make sure you understand how each marketing approach works and how it could benefit your own business. Then get ready to apply these techniques consistently and persistently—for as long as you are in business.

13

Developing Your Target Market

Before you can develop an appropriate marketing strategy, you need to identify and understand your target market (i.e., those most likely to need and, more importantly, *purchase* your product or service). First ask yourself three simple questions about the product or service you offer:

1. Who is it geared toward?
2. Who will it best serve?
3. Who will pay for it?

Identifying Your Market

Let's say you're going to start a tutoring service specializing in geometry and algebra or Spanish—or whatever your strongest subject is. Your target market? Parents of schoolchildren who are struggling in those classes. Then you can whittle the market down even further to include only those parents who are willing and able to pay for your services. *That* is your target market.

Or perhaps you live in a college town in which there is an obvious need for an excellent resumé service. You've decided to fill the void. Your target market? Graduating students who recognize their need for your service and can afford to pay for your expertise.

Once you identify your target market, you will need to know how to reach them. We wouldn't advise an interior designer to advertise in an apartment hunter's guide, for example. Renters who have no monetary investment in their home wouldn't be interested in that type of service.

In order to reach your target market, you need to know something about it. You should be able to identify certain characteristics common to many of your prospects. For example, do they depend on and read mail as a source of information, or are they likely to be more high-tech and cruise the Internet? Are they mobile and active? Do they earn sufficient income? Do they frequent the grocery store, the local library, the chamber of commerce? Would they have the time and inclination to attend seminars, lectures, or workshops you might offer as a marketing tool? Do they regularly read newspapers, magazines, or other publications?

Establishing a Niche

Research indicates that the most successful small businesses have carved out a niche for themselves by specializing to some degree within the line of products or services they offer. We recommend that you do the same; you can always broaden your focus later on if business is going well and you want to expand the services you offer.

What do we mean by "specialize"? Well, instead of offering a web-page design service to the world at large, your business specializes in creating sites for one type of client—realtors, for example. Or you are an accountant who specializes in construction companies or homeowners' associations.

You may think that by doing this you are narrowing your market too much, but it is much easier and more effective to market to an identifiable, homogeneous segment of the population. Why? Because your pool of prospects will share certain traits that you can capitalize on as you develop a marketing strategy. Plus, because you offer a specialized service, you can build a solid reputation as an expert in your field.

A Personal Glimpse   Jan Coffinberger started her business, J C Accounting Services, in 1991 so that she could stay home with her two young sons. Jan's first client was the neighborhood's swimming and tennis club—as it turned out, the "perfect client." At first, the work was cyclical. Her busiest period fell between February and June, when the club invoiced new and returning members and handled other accounting issues in preparation for the summer season. By the time the boys were home for their school vacation, the work had tapered off to a very manageable level. Because the pool was run by a board of volunteers Jan wasn't expected to be "on call" during the traditional 9:00 A.M.–5:00 P.M. work day as she would with a corporate client. This flexibility meant that she could do the work around the boys' schedules and when it suited her.

Jan soon realized that it would be easy to build an accounting business that specialized in recreational and community clubs. Most of these organizations were run more or less the same way, so the system she had already developed for her first account could easily be adapted for future clients. She had found her niche! Focusing on one type of client gave Jan an advantage when marketing to other organizations. After all, most people want to work with someone who knows *something* about what they do. Jan continues to grow her business marketing her services to similar organizations that, in turn, benefit from her specialized know-how.

A Personal Glimpse   Home-based mom and architect Rebecca Bostick had no trouble identifying a niche when she opened her own firm in 1989. Although the first two projects she worked on were a renovation and a house addition, her ultimate goal was to specialize in the design and renovation of schools, as she had done for her previous employer. As a mom she was interested in designing environments that would benefit children, and as a businesswoman she recognized the income potential. One school project every two years would provide enough "bread-and-butter income to keep the business going and feed the family." Any additional projects would be "gravy."

Despite fierce competition from other architectural firms, Rebecca won her first school project in 1991, and then bid successfully on two more soon afterward. Although she considers design and renovation of school buildings her niche, she has continued to complement that work with other projects. She has even used her non-school-based work to help her win the larger school projects; she recently clinched a $4.5 million job, in part because she included pictures of her home renovations in her presentation and impressed the decision makers with the quality of that aspect of her work. Rebecca has established a solid reputation and track record in her local school district and has begun to expand her focus and bid on projects in neighboring areas. Now expecting her third child, Rebecca recently finished her own addition—a new home office.

Here's a good example of identifying and reaching your target market:

Tanya started her business several years ago, in part because as a mother of two young children she was frustrated by the lack of a local facility where mothers and babies could go to meet, play, and network. She decided to fill the void and founded Toddlin' Time, a play gym for tots. Her target market? Moms at home, like her, with children ten months to four years old. How did she reach them? That was the easy part. Tanya put her marketing material wherever *she* went, for she was confident that's where the other moms went, too! She left her marketing materials at the grocery stores, the local library, the toy stores, the children's boutiques, the pediatrician's office, the playgrounds, and the park. She was also attuned to the many characteristics other moms shared: they probably read the same free weekly publication that arrived on Wednesday and stayed timely through the following week. Most lived on one income and had a fairly limited budget. They were likely to check and clip coupons and jump at a good deal whenever they ran across one.

Knowing what she knew about moms with small children and being able to predict their response to her prices and her program, Tanya was able to identify and reach her market successfully. As a result, her business grew steadily and quickly, and her client base tripled in its first year. Tanya knew her target market intimately because she happened to be a member of it. If your business is also geared toward moms and children, you will find it very easy to identify and reach potential customers. Simply ask yourself the same questions that Tanya did: "Where do *I* go for information?" "What do *I* rely on in print?" "What bulletin boards do *I* regularly check?" "Where do *I* go regularly?" and "What advertising material has worked on *me*?"

If you are starting a business in a market that is new to you, obviously you won't have the advantage of really knowing it well. Doing a little creative marketing research will help you initially until your own experience working with that market kicks in. Try conducting a survey by telephone or mail to elicit information that will help you tailor your marketing strategy to the needs of your market.

Another approach might be to seek out prospects that fit a certain profile and meet specific criteria you have established, such as income, lifestyle, etc. For example, your lawn and landscaping service will probably be of interest to single-family homeowners with medium- to large-size yards and with household incomes that fall within a certain range. Again, some of this information could be elicited from a survey, but another, less expensive alternative is to obtain demographic information about various communities from the media. Posing as a potential advertiser (who knows, you might decide to place an ad one day when business is really going well!), call your local or regional newspapers and radio and TV stations and ask them to send a media kit with demographic information. The media have the money to commission frequent surveys, and you'll be surprised how much information you can pick up about trends in your area.

Beating the Competition

Competition. Just saying the word can raise your stress level! What does it mean? What is a competitor? Basically, a competitor is someone who offers the same or similar product or service as you. In other words, it is someone who could very well be a threat to your business if the market is limited.

How do you overcome the competition? You need to be just a little more diligent, a little faster, a little friendlier, a little more flexible, a little less costly, or a little more flashy than they are. You need to find out what it is they do and do it differently—or better.

This is when you don your Sherlock Holmes hat and cape and, armed with your magnifying glass, head out to study and research the competition. Keep in mind that you are not out there to steal ideas, or duplicate another business. But you do need to know what your competitors are doing, how much they are charging, what services they offer, and so on. You also need to know what your competition is *not* doing. You can give your business added value by building in additional services or goodies. For example, if they don't offer free delivery, you should! If they charge an initial consultation fee, maybe you shouldn't, or at least make it less and then apply it as a down payment if you get the business. Are their prices too high? Undercut them slightly. Do they rarely offer coupons? Offer them regularly. There are a number of things you can do to encourage your target market to choose you over your competition.

How do you find out what it is your competition does or doesn't do? There are a few ways.

■ Ask friends who have used your competition to list the things they were satisfied with as well as the things they weren't pleased with. What would they like to see done differently in the future?

■ Posing as a customer, contact your competitors over the phone and inquire about their policies, prices, and customer-service guarantees. If there is anything you can improve on in your business, do so.

■ Take it a step further and actually use the product or service yourself and then be your own judge on how your business could offer your market just a little more. If you feel guilty about your undercover work, consider it necessary market research and bear in mind that as future businesses pop up, if they are smart, *you* will be the one under the magnifying glass.

You may (as unfortunate as it may be) from time to time hear that your competition is speaking negatively about you and your business. Don't, under any circumstances, stoop to their level and start dishing out insults in return. Instead, feel flattered that another business, possibly well established, feels threatened by you. Most customers will be able to make up their own mind as to which company offers the better product or service.

In some instances it may be to your benefit to try and befriend your competition, especially if it's another home-based mom like you. Some may be a bit apprehensive or suspicious about your friendly advances, but others will be responsive. They may be interested in exploring the idea of joining forces occasionally in order to fulfill a job that would be too big for either of you alone. They might even be interested in subcontracting work to you if they get overloaded, and vice versa. Just make sure you both understand your rights and responsibilities to each other and get it in writing! (See our section on contracts in Phase I.)

We have a motto that we think works. Put out the best possible product or service, one that you yourself would jump at because the quality is high, the price fair, and the service excellent, and customers will come. You will develop a list of faithful clients, and they will tell their friends about you. The last thing on your mind will be the competition.

Expanding Your Market

Once you have established a solid foundation for your business and your marketing efforts continue to bring in a steady, manageable flow of business, you may decide you are ready to expand your market a little. By this, we don't mean just growing your business bigger. Chances are you can continue to do that by building on your existing market(s). *Expanding* means finding a way to attract *additional* markets by developing or adding to your current product or service offering.

For example, following her successful first year with the gym, Tanya was ready to do just that. She had done well offering a service to stay-at-home moms, but she wanted to draw in working parents, too. Obviously, they weren't able to attend her weekday classes, so she had to come up with something else. Her solution? Offering birthday parties at the gym on weekends. The result? A successful expansion of her business that not only appealed to the new market she had identified but added an exciting new option that her existing clients could also benefit from.

Here are some suggestions for expanding your business:

■ Offer a workshop, demonstration, or lecture on your specialty. Attendees who didn't think they needed your services may be persuaded by your expertise that in fact they do!

■ If you teach, teach more. If you focus on teaching children a second language, consider offering a program for adults. If you teach adults dance, horseback riding, or some other recreational technique, consider developing a curriculum that would be suitable for children. Or offer mother-daughter and father-son sessions.

■ If you offer a service to big business, consider offering a scaled-down version to smaller businesses.

■ If you are a wedding planner, consider organizing private parties, sweet sixteens, bar and bat mitzvahs, communions, etc. Since all require careful planning but are not quite as rigorous or time-consuming as weddings, they can be fit in around the more intensive projects you are working on.

■ If you specialize in interior design, consider offering your services to small businesses as well as homeowners. Medical offices, restaurants, small hotels—even bed and breakfasts—could be candidates for your professional touch and may provide a more lucrative income stream for you.

Those are just a few ideas to get the wheels turning in the right direction. Of course, we can't give specific ideas for every type of business, but the general concepts mentioned here will apply to most. So get creative; adapt some of these ideas to your own situation and watch your business expand and grow!

Now that you have a basic idea about ways to identify and expand your target market, we're going to detail some of the promotional techniques that will help you reach it.

And so, "To market, to market…"

14

The ABCs of Effective Marketing

There are so many ways to market a business that first-time business owners may find it hard to decide which marketing tools and techniques will work best for them. There isn't necessarily a "right" way or a one-fits-all, so our "marketing menu" offers you a range of techniques that vary in cost and ease of preparation. As you consider the merits of each marketing tool, be guided by the type of business you own, the funds you have to work with, and the objective(s) you have set for yourself.

Setting Objectives

Establishing specific objectives and setting deadlines for achieving them will give you a starting point for your marketing efforts. After all, it's hard to know if you're making headway without goals to help you measure your progress. Your objectives don't need to be lofty or overly ambitious. Examples of objectives you might set are as follows:

- Find one new client by the end of the week.
- Sign up three new clients within two months.
- Make one thousand dollars year-end profit.
- Spend ten hours each week on marketing activities.

For each objective, draw up a detailed plan and check off the steps as you go.

Using a Marketing Plan

You may find that working on one marketing objective at a time is most comfortable for you or that you prefer the variety of working on several concurrently. Whichever approach works best for you, drawing up a plan of action for each objective will help organize your activities and give you a sense of your progress.

Let's look at an example. Angie offers a pet-sitting and grooming service and has established a reasonable customer base through word of mouth and by distributing fliers and promotional postcards around her local community. She is now ready to get a little more adventurous with her marketing endeavors. She sets an objective, gives herself a time frame, and establishes her plan.

Angie's plan also functions as a work sheet letting her check off the steps as they are completed. The Summary of Results section gives her a place to measure and record the ultimate success of her plan. You can use this plan, in conjunction with the information on various marketing techniques that follows, as a guideline to develop your own customized work sheets. Keep these work sheets together in a binder so that you can reference them easily and look back to see what has worked successfully for you.

Angie's Marketing Plan

MY OBJECTIVE: To add 5 new clients to my regular customer base

MY TIMEFRAME: 3 months

MY BUDGET: $200-$300

SOURCE(S) OF PROSPECTS:

1. Homeowner Association Directory

2. Mailing List from local vet's office(s)

3. Advertising Leads

MARKETING TOOLS:

1. Direct Mail brochure

2. Follow up postcard with discount offer

3. Classified ad in "Pets" section of local newspaper

PLAN OF ACTION:

Month 1
- ☐ Compile mailing list of 500 names from sources
- ☐ Mail brochure and business card to first 250 names
- ☐ Write classified ad and submit to newspapers for multiple insertions over 3 months

Month 2
- ☐ Mail follow up postcard to first 250 names
- ☐ Mail brochure and business card to second 250 names

Month 3
- ☐ Mail follow up postcard to second 250 names

SUMMARY OF RESULTS:

_____

_____

_____

Marketing Plan Worksheet

MY OBJECTIVE: _____

MY TIMEFRAME: _____

MY BUDGET: _____

SOURCE(S) OF PROSPECTS:

1. _____

2. _____

3. _____

4. _____

MARKETING TOOLS:

1. _____

2. _____

3. _____

4. _____

PLAN OF ACTION

1. _____

2. _____

3. _____

4. _____

SUMMARY OF RESULTS

_____

_____

_____

The Tool Kit

Fliers

Fliers are quick and inexpensive to produce, and if you succeed in getting them into the hands of your potential clients, they can be a very effective marketing tool. At a cost of three or four cents per flier, you will quickly recoup your investment if your distribution is successful and brings in just a few new customers.

Fliers should be fun, creative, and eye-catching. In fact, if you have access to a computer, you will find software that practically does the job for you. If you don't have your own computer, hire a graphic designer or desktop publisher (depending on your budget!) to design it for you.

Fliers can be posted on bulletin boards, left in a stack at appropriate locations, hand-delivered, or mailed in bulk to businesses or residences. (See our section on bulk mailing later on.) If you are operating on a strict budget, fliers are a good way to get word out about your business. If you are marketing to businesses, attach a business card to the fliers and deliver them personally. Doing so will give you a chance to ask for a contact name and also make a good impression on the prospect.

You will want to make sure you include the following information in your flier:

- Your business name
- Your logo
- Your phone number
- The features and benefits of the product or service you offer
- An incentive, such as a discount coupon or expiration date on a sale or special, to help create a sense of urgency

Ask friends and family members to look at your flier and then give you some feedback. Would they stop and read it? Would it stand out on a bulletin board? Would they feel inclined to call you for further information about your business? If the answer is no, go back to the drawing table and ask yourself what you can do to jazz it up a bit. A different font? More graphics? A larger logo? Some color? Playing around with the design can give your flier a whole new look and give you a better chance of getting business from it.

Once you have a finished product but before you have copies made, proofread—and proofread again. Ask someone who hasn't seen it yet to proofread it for you, too. You want to make sure that there are no typing errors, that your business name and logo appear clean and clear, and that your phone number is correct. (You'll kick yourself if you find out five hundred fliers later that you transposed the last two digits of your phone number. Your fliers will only have one destination in that case—the "round file"!)

As always, call around for competitive pricing when you are ready to have your flier printed. Chances are you'll find that the office-supply store or local copy shop can give you a good price on a small print run. Pick a brightly colored paper for maximum eye appeal and impact even if it costs a fraction more than plain white stock.

Now that you have the fliers, they will only get you business if you distribute them—as widely as possible.

Do put your fliers in

- Grocery stores.
- Libraries.
- Community centers.
- Local gyms; they usually have a bulletin board posted in the lobby or locker room or you may be able to leave them at the reception area.
- Preschools and child-care centers.
- Church bulletin boards.
- Point-of-sale counters at specialty stores that relate to your business.
- College-campus bulletin boards.
- Cafeterias or delicatessens that have bulletin boards for the use of their customers.

- Hand-delivered to business prospects with your business card attached.

However, so as not to waste your valuable marketing tool

- Don't leave them on parked cars in parking lots. Most drivers find this extremely annoying, and many will trash your flier without even taking a glance. Worse still, they will end up on the ground as litter—not a good image for your business.
- Don't put them in out-of-the way places where they won't be seen easily.
- Don't put them in places that your target market will rarely or never visit.
- Don't leave outdated fliers on display, especially if they are time-sensitive and include an expiration date for an offer you are running. Replace them with new fliers and recycle the old ones as scratch paper or drawing paper for the kids.
- Don't put your fliers in mailboxes. This is viewed as a violation by the U.S. Postal Service, and you may be fined. Instead, put fliers in door handles or in newspaper boxes.

Make a list of where you plan to distribute your fliers and where you think they will do best. Take the list with you on your distribution run and check off each place and the approximate number of fliers you left there. This will help you keep track of the places where your fliers are seen and picked up most. Make sure you get permission before leaving fliers at each location. It will be a waste of your time and money if your carefully crafted fliers are thrown away simply because you didn't ask for permission before leaving them.

Make up a "flier response" log sheet, and when a call comes in from a flier you've posted or delivered, always ask the caller where they saw the information and record it in your log. Then, when you are ready to put out more materials, you'll know which locations worked best for you and brought in the most responses.

Fliers can be a great way for certain types of businesses to reach clients for just a little bit of money. Remember, be creative. Try to capture the attention of your potential clients and the result can be a business line that rings often. And *that* can be a wonderful sound!

Brochures

A brochure is more complex than a flier because it is usually folded. It therefore needs to be organized differently. Your brochure will allow you to communicate more information about your business than a business card or flier. Whatever your budget, you can probably come up with a smart brochure that does a good job for you.

Brochures come in various sizes and configurations but most commonly will be on letter-or legal-sized paper which is folded into thirds or fourths, giving you six to eight panels with which to work. If you want to use your brochures as self-mailers, you will need to leave one panel blank for a mailing label.

As a marketing tool, you will want your brochure to provide prospects with as much information as possible to help them make the decision to do business with you. The focus should be to highlight the features and benefits of the product or service you offer, and the goal is to leave a strong, positive impact about your business.

At the very least, include the following information:

- A brief history of your company, why and how you started it, and if appropriate, information about you and your credentials
- The features and benefits of the product or service you provide
- Your company logo, mailing address, phone and fax numbers
- Favorable comments/references from satisfied clients
- Preferably a photo or some kind of graphic to illustrate what you are offering or just to break up the text

Use the best type of paper you can afford, and if possible, use more than one color ink. Nowadays it's possible to buy attractive, colorful brochure paper through mail order or even from your local copy

Features and Benefits

When selling your product or service to a prospective customer, make him or her aware of two things:

1. The *features* of your product or service
2. The *benefits* of your product or service

For example, Sally's Kids Klothing manufactures and sells a line of all-natural, easy-wear, easy-care clothing for babies and toddlers. The *features* of the garments are as follows:

- They have easy-release snaps in the diaper area.
- They have adjustable straps at the shoulder.
- They are made from all-natural, soft cotton.
- They are machine washable and tumble dryable.

Although your prospects may be able to see the features very clearly for themselves, sometimes it will be up to you to point out the benefits before you can win their business. The corresponding *benefits* are as follows:

- You can change baby's diaper easily without totally undressing him.
- The adjustable straps mean the outfit will grow with baby, giving you months more wear.
- The natural fibers will not irritate baby's soft skin.
- Ease of care and laundering saves you time.

store. All you need to do is run them through your printer, and voilà! Instant brochures! Just make sure that the color scheme ties in with the rest of your stationery. You'll be sending out presentation packets at some point, and you'll want your materials to look coordinated.

Finally, don't have brochures printed with any information that is likely to change. For example, rather than include a price list in the brochure itself, have a separate price sheet printed on matching paper that you can slip in between the folds of the brochure. This way, if your prices change, you won't have to reprint an entire batch of brochures. On the same note, if your address is likely to change, consider a more permanent alternative and rent a post-office box or leave space for a clear label with your return address on it.

Postcards

Everyone has time to read a postcard; a few lines about an upcoming event, an open house, a seminar, lecture, or function can be absorbed at a glance. With no envelope to open and no paper to unfold, a postcard mailing can often be as effective, if not more so, than a letter. As always, however, it must look professional and attractive.

You have much less room on a typical 5 ½-by-4 ¼ inch postcard than on a flier, and you only have one side to work with. So to avoid an overcrowded look, you will want to condense the text to a bare minimum. Make sure that the most important information is in larger, bolder type. If you have trouble fitting everything or you want to include an attractive graphic, consider using a larger, oversized postcard for maximum impact.

Once you have your copy prepared, your local printer can paste it up and run off as many copies as you need on a heavier card stock that will stand up to being mailed alone. (If you had planned to print the whole thing yourself, bear in mind that many of the card stocks won't run through your laser printer.) Find out if your printer charges extra for cutting the cards; you could save money on this step by using a paper cutter to do it yourself.

Note: See our example of a promotional postcard on page 200.

Coupons

We clip them, we save them, we stuff them in our purse, and we use them. And the good news is, so do a lot of others. A coupon is nothing more than an incentive to do business with you, and people love incentives. It is an effective way to motivate someone to try your product or service for the first time. If they are pleased with what they get from you, they will continue to come back for more.

There's nothing new about using coupons to attract and keep customers, but nowadays it's been made very easy, thanks to coupon cooperatives, to get coupons into the hands of consumers. These companies are in business for the sole purpose of bundling coupons from several different organizations into one consolidated packet which is then sent out en masse to thousands and thousands of consumers. Their end product ends up in our mailboxes at least once or twice each week.

Are coupon cooperatives expensive? At a minimum of three hundred to four hundred dollars for each mailing, at first glance it may seem so. After all, you want to spend your marketing dollars wisely. But most coupon cooperatives profess to reach some ten thousand homes, often more. If your target market is the local community and you can reach that many prospects in one shot, it doesn't seem quite so expensive anymore. Even at the post office's lowest mail rate, the postage alone would be prohibitively expensive for most small businesses to consider a mailing of this size. And if only 1 percent respond, you'll still have a hundred interested prospects to work with!

As with all your print materials, your coupon will conjure up an image of your company to those it reaches. The most effective coupons are well designed and offer a strong incentive for people to use them. Here are some tips:

▪ Make sure your coupon is well designed. You will have the opportunity to approve it before it is printed and distributed, so proof it carefully. As always, your logo, business name, and telephone number should be clear and easy to read. Make the information stand out by using bold, large type and make sure that the incentive or discount you are offering really grabs attention.

▪ Choose the coupon company carefully. Pick a company that has been in business for a while and is reputable. Ask the representative to show you *exactly* the format and design of the distribution packet your coupon will go into so that you know what to expect.

■ Make your incentive worthwhile so that it is very appealing and makes your coupon worth keeping. Sometimes a few dollars off just isn't incentive enough. Ask yourself what *you* would consider *too good to pass up* and then offer it. Remember, the hard part is winning a client's business the first time. Once they're "hooked," the excellence of your product or service will keep them coming back, so the incentive need only be offered once. (Make sure your coupon clearly states "for new customers only" if you are using it only to attract more clients.)

■ Always include an expiration date on your coupon. This will create a sense of urgency and motivate people to use it before it is out-of-date.

■ Add color to your coupon if possible. Sometimes for a little more money you can get a color or a combination of colors put into your design. The more eye-catching the coupon, the more likely people are to read it.

■ If you receive a positive response after running a coupon, adjust your marketing budget so that you can run it again in the near future. Anytime a marketing tool works well to bring in new business, it should go to the top of your list and get priority when you're allocating funds.

■ Ask the coupon company for exclusivity. In other words, request that no other type of business similar to yours be included in the packet. You may be told that they cannot make that guarantee, but it can't hurt to ask.

■ If the cost is simply too much for you to manage, ask if you can share a coupon with another business. Some coupon companies offer this option, and it can literally cut your costs in half.

If possible, print off several of your own coupons and leave them at various places along with, or instead, of fliers. A stack of coupons might be just the perfect thing to leave at a place of business when there is no room for the larger fliers.

Coupons aren't appropriate or cost-effective for every type of business, but if you think they might work for you, give them a try. As long as people keep stashing them and cashing them in, coupons will bring in new customers—and that's the way your business will grow.

Newsletters

Publishing and mailing a complimentary newsletter to clients, prospects, and other contacts can be a very effective marketing tool. It's a relatively inexpensive way to stay in touch with your existing customers and impress prospects with your expertise and knowledge.

For example, Laurie operates a computer-repair service and, as a courtesy, endeavors to keep her regular customers updated with information on the latest technological developments. She decides to use a newsletter as a vehicle do to this and creates *Bits 'n Bytes*, a two-sided bimonthly publication filled with helpful information for computer users. She doesn't have to do any special research; she culls most of the information from the publications that she reads, anyway, to keep up on her trade. She includes tips on maximizing computer performance, reviews of new software products, and a Q & A column in which she answers common computer-related questions and concerns.

Her clients like the newsletter because it shortcuts some of the research they would normally have to do, and by keeping her name in front of them in a positive way, Laurie is guaranteed of future business.

A newsletter doesn't have to be a long, complicated document; in fact, when you are using it primarily as a marketing tool, you want to keep it short and snappy. A two- or four-sided newsletter, folded in half or thirds, will give you enough space to include enough information and still give you a panel you can use for the mailing label. But remember, as with all your other printed materials, spend some time on the initial design and layout. A poorly designed piece will erode your credibility rather than enhance it. If you can afford it, add some color. Talk to your printer about preprinting a "shell" with your masthead, company name, etc., on which you can then print the newsletters each time.

Keep the content informational and focused. Above all, avoid the temptation to make the content too "salesy" or your credibility will be questioned.

Mail your newsletter not only to existing clients but to prospects, vendors, and other networking and trade contacts. Your newsletter should pay for itself with leads and new business it generates.

Trade Shows

They are fun to participate in, a great avenue for networking, and potentially a good marketing tool. There is a trade show, or shows, appropriate for just about every conceivable business type, and they have the advantage of bringing you directly in contact with your target market.

Trade shows are usually organized and run by a single company—an events planner who is also responsible for all the preshow marketing and promotion. Your job is to portray your business in the best possible light in the space you are allotted—generally based on how much you pay for it.

Trade shows can be expensive. Even small shows will probably charge what may seem to be an exorbitant fee. For this you may get nothing more than a table and a few feet of space to display your wares. Usually you are offered a range of more elaborate settings and price levels if you are willing to pay more.

But, by using some creativity and imagination, you can absolutely maximize the space you are occupying no matter how humble it seems! Here's how:

- Well before the show, find out the dimensions of your table and the space surrounding it. Find out what the show will provide you in the way of tablecloth, company sign, access to electrical outlets, etc., and plan from there. Think of ways you can design a placard or some other type of sign that will draw people's eye and bring them over for a closer look.

- Consider doing a premailing to existing customers and your prospect list, inviting them to stop by your booth. This is a good time to consider a postcard mailing.

- Have plenty of marketing material on hand to give out. Brochures, business cards, and/or information sheets about your business should be easily accessible for people to pick up when they stop by.

- Hold a drawing for a free product or service. People love the chance to win something. Have a stack of small forms available with space for a name, address, and telephone number. Since these are filled out and entered into the drawing, you will also get yourself an instant mailing list! Although most trade shows provide exhibitors with a list of attendees after the event, it could take several weeks or even months before it is compiled and mailed out to you. In the meantime, you will be a step ahead and can begin marketing to these potential clients immediately.

- Have the name of your company and your logo in as many areas of your booth as possible.

- If possible, create a colorful, creative pictorial display that clearly shows the benefits of your product or service. Some people relate to images far better than to text. Design your display vertically with some height so that passersby will be able to see it over the crowd if your booth is busy.

- If you manufacture or sell a product, make sure you have several samples on display so that your potential customers can see, touch, and feel them! If appropriate, have small sample packets made up and hand them out. Take a cash box and plenty of small change so that you don't have to turn customers away for lack of it! *Note:* If you find that a trade show is the ideal venue for selling your product, consider applying for merchant status so that you can accept credit cards. This may make it easier for your customers to make a buying decision, for we all know it's easier to hand over that card than a wad of cash! (See Obtaining Merchant Status, page 69.)

- Find out in advance just where your table or booth will be located. If you can, ask to be placed near an entrance. If you aren't happy with your position in the show, express your concerns and ask to be moved. Remember, the squeaky wheel gets the oil!

- Ask the organizers for exclusivity; that is, that they agree that no other companies in your line of business will be able to participate. Your request might be turned down, but you may be able to negotiate something if you are willing to pay for the privilege.

- Put your best face forward on the day of the show. Try to get a decent amount of sleep the night before the show. Arrange for a babysitter that day; you will not want to be chasing small children around when you should be manning your booth. Arrive in plenty of time to set up your booth before the show starts and wear comfortable shoes; trade shows can be hard on the feet! Finally, be personable and smile often. Don't always wait for people to come up to you. Welcome them with a smile and ask them if they'd like to enter your drawing or hear a little more about your product or service.

- Use the opportunity to do some good networking. Trade shows are great places to make new contacts and solidify existing ones. Make sure you take the time to "do the rounds." You may be able to pick up helpful information and check up on your competition at the same time.

- If a trade show is simply out of the question for you because of the cost, ask the organizers if, as an alternative to buying a table, you can pay a token amount for a small display of your brochures and business cards. An unmanned networking table may be made available for this purpose if enough businesses request it.

You can find out about upcoming trade shows in your area through your local papers, periodicals that relate to your trade, networking functions, and your local chamber of commerce. Companies that organize these shows usually begin marketing for exhibitors several months before the actual show.

You may participate in a trade show and not see or feel the results until several weeks or months later. Sometimes it just serves as another avenue for exposure as well as an elaborate networking function. Ask yourself if you can afford to be in a local trade show. If your competitors are going to be present, can you afford not to?

A Personal Glimpse   Paula Fargo has been a regular trade-show exhibitor since becoming a Discovery Toys (DT) consultant 12½ years ago. Now a sterling manager and multimedia consultant (someone who sells multimedia software and games), Paula has built an impressive sales team of consultants—a growth she attributes, in part, to her active participation on the trade-show circuit.

Paula learned early on that to make the most of a trade show you have to go into it with the right attitude: "Attitude is everything, and you have to be realistic about your expectations. You're not going to sell thousands of dollars' worth of inventory at a trade show, but it *is* a great place to make contacts." Paula also approaches each event in a very businesslike manner. She "rents" space at her exhibit table to other DT consultants to help cover expenses, often sets up play areas at no charge, and even runs workshops on topics such as learning styles or choosing children's software. And she arrives each day ready to be "energetic, positive, and upbeat. I've never understood why someone would pay eight hundred dollars for exhibitor space and then just sit behind the table and read a book!"

Paula admits that she has experienced mixed success with trade shows. She has found, for example, that the largest, most expensive events aren't necessarily the best venues for her. Often there's some trial and error before you can be confident that an event will be beneficial to your business. But the bottom line for Paula is that trade shows have helped her build her business, brought her many helpful contacts, honed her sales skills, and continue to play a large role in her marketing efforts.

Direct Mail

Direct mail simply means sending a promotional or informational marketing piece through the mail to either your own mailing list, compiled over time from your own clients and prospects, or a mailing list you have acquired from another source. Of course, you can always do both.

Either way, when you mail your marketing message directly to a list of individuals who have expressed interest in your business activity or at least fit the profile of those who should, you are mailing to "qualified prospects"—and that's a good thing!

Hopefully, you will have some way of computerizing your in-house mailing list, which will make printing address labels relatively easy and automatic.

But assuming that your current in-house mailing list isn't really extensive enough to support a *large* promotional mail campaign, there are generally two ways to obtain an outside mailing list.

The first way is to get it directly from an organization that targets your market itself and makes its list available for rent to other companies. You can also get it from a list compiler—a company that specializes in building huge databases of names and addresses from all over the country. (You can find one or more of these companies under the category "Mailing Lists" in your telephone's yellow pages.) The powerful software used by these operations can sort through millions of entries to provide you with an extremely "targeted" list that meets the criteria you specify.

For example, ABC Toys is a mail-order company selling children's toys, books, and educational software geared toward the under-twelve-year-old market. Their target market is parents of children under twelve, and so they could rent lists from any number of sources: for example, national parenting magazines, other mail-order companies targeting the same market, toy retailers, etc. ABC could assume that the lists rented would be relatively "qualified," since patrons of one list would be interested in ABC's offerings also.

But another alternative for ABC would be to obtain a more targeted mailing list directly from a list compiler, which would allow them to "customize" the mailing by specifying that only names meeting specific criteria should be included on the list, such as:

- Income level between $50,000 and $75,000
- Children between the ages of two and twelve
- Defined Zip code(s) that fall within a specific UPS (United Parcel Service) mailing district

By selecting their list this way, ABC might receive fewer responses to their mailing, but they would probably end up with more sales because the list was more targeted.

When you "outsource" your list, you have the choice of paying for preprinted labels for a one-time-only mailing or purchasing the names on an electronic medium which will give you unlimited use of the list. Most marketing experts acknowledge that repetition is key in an effective direct-mail campaign, so it's probably sensible to plan for at least two to three mailings, if not more.

What Will You Send?

You can send out any of your marketing pieces in a direct-mail promotion—fliers, postcards, brochures, coupons, newsletters, and so on. You might want to include a reply card that interested prospects can fill out and send back for more information. Including an incentive offer along with a "reply-by" date will motivate them to respond more quickly. Make sure that your business phone number is also prominently displayed for those that are sufficiently motivated to call for more information.

If you are in manufacturing and/or sales, you might be using direct mail to send out catalogs, product order forms, and so on. If your goal is to generate orders for the product or products you sell, your mailer will have to be detailed enough that recipients can make a buying decision based purely on the mail piece. It will also need to include ordering and shipping information.

Using a Mailing Service

When your mailing is small—anything from a couple of hundred to a couple of thousand pieces—you might opt to do it all yourself. But if you're sending out thousands of pieces, think about hiring a service to do it for you. Even if you recruit your children as helpers, folding, stuffing, labeling, and sorting thousands of pieces of paper can be a horribly intimidating task that will take over your life for a while!

A mailing service will take the whole thing off your hands—for a price, obviously! But you can instruct your printer to send the printed pieces directly to the mailing service. They will then take care of folding (if the printer didn't already do that, get prices from both places before you assign that task), stuffing, labeling, and sorting to conform to the post office's strict bulk-mail regulations. What's more, most mailing services have their own bulk permit, so you don't have to bother with that step, although you will have to prepay the postage.

Doing It Yourself—Using Bulk Mail

Mailing services are great because they have invested in the equipment necessary to deal with huge quantities of paper, but if your mailing is a manageable size, you will no doubt want to save money and do it yourself. Assuming you are mailing more than two hundred pieces on a fairly regular basis, the most cost effective method for doing this is to use the post office's bulk-mail rate.

The post office offers a third-class-mail option to companies that want to reach a large number of consumers with more or less the same mail piece. You used to call it "junk mail," but now that you are considering using it, "bulk mail" is a much friendlier term!

If you want to use bulk mail, you will have to obtain a permit from the post office to do so. The post office will charge you an annual fee to retain your bulk-mail privileges, and there may be additional fees, depending on how and what you intend to mail. Contact your local post office or postal business center for specific information. Before making the investment, however, bear in mind the following:

- Using bulk mail will only be cost-effective if you send out several mailings each year that are at least two hundred pieces each.
- What you save in money you will spend in time if you do the mailing yourself. Even if you subcontract the folding, stuffing, and labeling, there are several levels of address sorts you will have to perform to conform to bulk-mail requirements. (Caroline bulk-mailed her newsletter, *ConneXions*, for several years and can attest to the fact that it is time-consuming, tedious, and messy!)
- Just as *you* sometimes discard bulk mail without even looking at it, your mail piece may be destined for the same fate! (See previous

tips on design.) Also, if you are mailing a time-sensitive piece, plan ahead, because bulk mail always takes longer than first-class mail to reach its destination.

Advertising

Advertising can be tricky for small businesses—and costly if you make a mistake. Some well-placed ads can be an extremely effective method of promoting your business, but you may not be able to put enough of your marketing dollars into advertising to make it worthwhile.

Opportunities for advertising, both print and broadcast, aren't in short supply. Between national and local newspapers, trade journals, magazines, newsletters, radio, TV, and cable, you might be overwhelmed by choices if it weren't for one very significant factor: *cost*. For most of us, the costlier media are well beyond any realistic budget, so we will be concentrating on the lower-priced options— that is, print ads—in this section. You'll read about some other creative ways to participate in the expensive media later on!

First, decide how much you can afford to spend. Generally, a series of smaller, lower-cost ads will be more successful than one big, splashy ad. Research suggests that people generally don't act the first or even the second time they are exposed to an advertisement. It is when they are continually exposed to an ad (and/or other promotional materials from the same business) that they may finally be spurred into action. The exception to this might be when a publication is running a supplement that is specifically geared to your audience and so provides you with a very targeted advertising opportunity. For example, that single splashy ad in a special wedding supplement of your local newspaper would be worthwhile if you are a wedding planner, a florist, a photographer, or catering to the wedding industry in some way.

Once you have a budget in mind, you'll need to decide where your dollars will work best for you. Consider which media makes the most sense for your business. What do your prospective clients read or see? If your business is strictly local, a local newspaper ad campaign might do the trick. However, if you sell mail-order gardening tools, a national homes-and-gardens publication might bring you more business.

Contact the advertising departments of publications which meet your marketing criteria and ask for an advertising-media kit and rate card. Most kits contain information regarding circulation, distribution, and demographic information about the publication's readers. This will help you zero in on the right place to put your advertising.

Now for the unpleasant part—figuring out what size ad and how many times you can afford to run it without busting your budget! Generally, the publications that generate the most subscribers or can show the biggest circulation charge the most for advertising—with one caveat. Some *specialty* publications may not have a huge circulation but can charge relatively more for advertising simply because their readership is so "targeted."

Most newspapers and magazines offer a choice of display or classified advertising: "Display" advertising tends to appear in the body of the publication and is sold by the size of the space it occupies. "Classified" advertising is organized under headings by category, as in, for example, "For Sale," "Business Services," "Tutoring Services," and the price is determined by the number of words the ad contains. Classified will almost always cost less than display advertising and in some cases may be more effective.

Classified ads can often be placed over the telephone or faxed to the publication. You will be able to give your ad a heading to catch the reader's eye: UPGRADE YOUR COMPUTER or MATH MADE EASY. Remember, if they are looking in the classifieds under a particular category heading, then they are probably looking for what you offer, so they are already what we call "qualified prospects."

Display advertising requires a little more preparation. You have more space to fill and the option to include a graphic or illustration of some sort. You don't have to actually design the ad yourself. The publication will put it together and fax you a proof for review. But it's probably worth spending the time and money to have a professional ad design done that you can use in various publications at different times. Or have a camera-ready "shell" designed that can be customized to reflect different product offerings or special promotions you are running. If you do use your own art, make sure you leave enough time to get it to the publication before its deadline.

Here are a few other things to remember about placing an advertisement:

- Ask the ad rep if you can get a lower price by purchasing a multiple-insertion contract. *Note:* Make sure that you can cancel without being obligated to fulfill the entire contract if response to your ad is poor. You should only have to pay the difference between the contract price and the one-off price for the ads that have already run.

- Make sure the ad includes:
  —Your company name
  ·—Your logo
  —Your phone number
  —Any incentive or discount offering
  —Product or service information, including price if appropriate
  —Fax number, E-mail, and mailing address if you have room

- Don't take out an ad that is so small it will get lost in the paper. Anything much smaller than a business card won't have much impact.

- Ask to have your ad placed in the section most likely to reach your target market. For example, if you are selling a line of cooking utensils, ask to be placed in the "Food" section, and so on.

- Ask the ad rep whether your ad will appear in all regional editions of the publication or if you can negotiate a better rate by requesting limited distribution in your key areas of operation.

- If you are still unsure about committing to an ad in a particular publication, consider contacting some of the businesses that have advertised in it. Ask them if the response to their ads lived up to expectations.

Finally, remember that there are many ways to end up in a newspaper or magazine that won't cost you much more than paper and postage. Read on.

A Personal Glimpse   Laurie Wrigley and Sharon St. Pierre have been friends since meeting at a play group six years ago with their firstborns. Between them they had attended their share of birthdays in so-called fun centers, where the children often ended up overwhelmed by the noise and commotion or, worse yet, separated from the rest of the birthday group. So, putting their creative talents to work, the two, now with three children each, formed Boxed Birthdays Company, "with the goal of making it easy for parents to host a personalized party that is affordable, fun, and educational." The boxes include everything necessary to host a fun theme party at home—invitations, paper goods, party-favor bags, and activity guides—and are, in fact, mailed directly to the hosting family's home.

Once they had the basic premise in place, Laurie and Sharon spent five months getting ready to "go live." They researched and made arrangements to buy products from wholesalers; developed twenty party themes, such as Pirates, Land of the Dinosaurs, Fairy Princess, Dalmatian Puppies, and more; took care of "all the legal stuff we had to do; and put in an accounting system."

Once all the basics were taken care of, they turned their attention to marketing and decided on a multipronged approach to "kick off" their business. (*Note:* See "the five tool rule" on page 211.)

"We started advertising in local family newspapers, and at the same time we exhibited at a local family expo, which was good, because we started to build our mailing list from that. We also offered the birthday boxes as fund-raisers at different preschools; for every box we sold we donated five dollars to the school. We also purchased a mail list. We targeted parents with children, ages one through twelve, with the income level we wanted within certain Zip codes. We were also able to get this information sorted by the children's month of birth, which was great, because we could time a mailer to arrive two months or so before the birthday."

Laurie and Sharon also launched a press campaign, sending press releases to the local print and broadcast media that resulted in some coverage of their new enterprise. "We found that the press releases were a very nice, free way to market. It was basically free advertising."

The final part of their marketing plan was to go "high tech" and experiment with a website. Despite being experimental, the success of the online marketing really surprised both partners. "It was really amazing to us, as it's ended up being about half of our business. We're also able to sell nationally and internationally through the Internet. We just sent a package to Oman which was really neat! In fact, it's been so successful that we upgraded our website this past spring."

In fact, Boxed Birthdays has done so well during its first year of operation that Laurie and Sharon have been inundated with requests that they offer distributorships, and they are currently researching the possibilities of expanding that way.

A creative, quality product, good service, and smart marketing have made the Boxed Birthdays Company a marketing success story.

15

Becoming Your Own PR Director

It would be wonderful if we all started our home-based businesses with a large chunk of change to devote strictly to marketing. Unfortunately, most of us don't have that luxury and need to come up with some creative ways to market on a shoestring, at least in the beginning. All the marketing methods we have looked at thus far require some financial outlay, and although most of them are relatively inexpensive, you may find you can only afford one or two, and that simply isn't enough to get your business the exposure it deserves.

But it is possible to supplement, or even replace, the marketing tools discussed earlier with one or more of the "shoestring" strategies that follow. See how innovative you can be with some of these ideas!

Using the Media to Your Advantage

In the previous section we talked about various media—print and broadcast—and acknowledged that most of the more widely seen, heard, or read media channels would be way beyond most of our budgets. But there are other ways to obtain the extensive coverage these media provide—without paying for it!

How? By giving the media a reason to publish or broadcast your information—generally by sending them a document called a press release. We're going to talk about two different types of publicity that a press release can generate to benefit your business: (1) a business or informational announcement; (2) a feature article or TV or radio appearance highlighting your business.

Informational Business Announcements

From the day you start your business, the media can be instrumental in publicizing it, starting with an announcement that you are open for business. Later on, you may want to publicize a class or seminar or make an announcement about some other business-related activity. Whatever you want to publicize, notify the press and your announcement could end up in print.

The way you present your information to the press is crucial. Long-winded, friendly letters describing your business in detail are *out*! Short, succinct paragraphs with just the facts are *in*! A newsroom is a busy, hustling place that doesn't have time for details; they have time to read a paragraph, and that's how long your press release should be. See our sample to help you make your own.

Cooking With Class

announces...

NEWS RELEASE

Cooking with Class will hold a workshop on Saturday, January 23rd, and Sunday, January 24th from 1 pm to 4 pm at the public library on 123 Oak Street.

The seminar is free and will introduce attendees to the classic cuisine and culinary delights of France. Samples provided.

Call 555-1234 for further information.

This is an effective press release because it is informative, short, and to the point. There is no mistaking that it is a press release because of the big, bold heading, and the chances of it being read and included in a calendar listing are very good. Make sure you send a press release out two to three weeks before the scheduled event and then another one seven to ten days prior. Most media require that kind of lead time.

Feature Article or TV/Radio Appearance

There's nothing like a full-blown article, complete with pictures, in a local or national publication or an appearance on the local television news to give you and your business instant credibility. Better yet, good publicity frequently boosts business for the lucky recipient. But how do you convince the media that your business is worth featuring? Obviously it will take more than the informational press release mentioned above.

You'll need to send out a more detailed press release (but again, preferably one page in length and certainly no more than two) along with any other relevant information and, if available, reprints of other articles that have been published about you. Editors and producers are often persuaded to develop features about topics that they can see have already generated some media interest.

This is where you get creative! You'll need to come up with a unique "hook," or angle, and build your press release around it. Here are some ideas:

- Exploit any upcoming event or holiday that somehow relates to your business. It seems as though there is a national "day" for just about everything these days, so you're sure to be able to come up with something!
- Anything that is unique and unusual about your business. For example, if your business is the first of its kind in your area or there is something unusual about the way you are operating it.
- Topicality. The media climb on certain bandwagons at certain

times; you may be able to capitalize on their existing interest in a specific topic.

- Being a home-based business mom. It's topical, it's interesting, and in itself it's sometimes enough to inspire media interest.

Don't be disappointed if your first release isn't picked up immediately; it may take several phone calls, letters, or further press releases before an editor takes a look at what you have to offer and considers its strength as a story. The key is to keep trying.

You have a couple of options when it comes to contacting the media.

Phone First   If you enjoy "cold calling" and find the phone a great way to establish contact, call and try to pique the reporter's interest in your story. Your "script" could go something like this:

"Hello. My name is _____ from _____ [your business name]. We are a new business in the area and the focus of our [product/service] is _____. The response we've received since opening for business in _____ [month opened] seems to indicate that there was a real need for this service in our community, and we wanted to make you aware of what we are all about. We think our business would make a great story!"

The reporter may take the time to talk to you immediately or ask for your media kit. Either way, you have made a contact. Make a note of whom you spoke to and send out a media kit the same day.

Mail Your Information   In order to save money and time on the phone, consider doing a mass mailing to several media contacts, introducing your business in such a way that it seems newsworthy and topical. In this case, you probably don't want to make follow-up phone calls, but consider including a Rolodex card with your company name, telephone number, your name, and a one- or two-line reminder that briefly describes your business.

Media-Kit Checklist

- Press release.
- Good-quality photograph(s).
- Brochure.
- Fact sheet and biographical information, if appropriate.
- Press clippings or good-quality reprints, including name of publication and date published.
- Business and/or Rolodex cards for reporters' files.
- Testimonials.
- Press pass if you are publicizing an event, but don't hold your breath for the press to show up!

Make sure that everything is on your stationery and is enclosed in an attractive presentation folder.

Press releases follow a fairly standard format, which makes it easy to devise your own, even if you've never done it before.

- Typed, double-spaced with wide margins, 1 to 1½ inches all around.

- Make sure your company name and address are prominently at the top. (Your company letterhead will probably work fine.)

- Include the name and phone number of a contact so that the reporter can follow up.

- Always put a release date. If it's not time-sensitive, put *release at will,* or if it is about an upcoming event and needs to be read by a certain date, use wording *for release* (date).

- Come up with an attention-grabbing headline that will catch an editor's eye.

- Use crisp, clear prose and don't be afraid to talk up your company or yourself; this is no time for humility! If you find it hard to talk about yourself in glowing terms, ask a friend to help you out.

Caroline Hull

MONEYMAKING
MOMS
How Work at Home Can Work For You

Tanya Wallace

PRESS RELEASE

Contact:703/555-1234
Caroline Hull *or*
Tanya Wallace

Contact name
and tel. #

<u>For Immediate Release</u>

"Hook"/Bold Heading

Entrepreneurial Moms Share Secrets of Home-based Business Success

Manassas, Virginia. January 2, 1998.

Origination point & date

With eight young children between them, you might think that entrepreneurial moms Caroline

Hull and Tanya Wallace had their hands full already. But the indefatigable pair claim to have

found the perfect way to balance family and career – by bringing their work home. Recognizing

the need many moms have for a more balanced life, Hull and Wallace have teamed up to share

their secrets for success with the growing number of moms interested in this solution to the

juggling act.   **Wide margins/
                                                                double spaced**

<u>Moneymaking Moms: How Work at Home Can Work for You</u> is a how-to-manual which gives

busy moms step-by-step instruction and advice on building and growing a business from home.

<u>Moneymaking Moms</u> etc. etc. etc.

Hull and Wallace both chose to start their home-based businesses in order to spend time with

their children – Hull has five children ages thirteen, twelve (twins), eight, and three. Wallace's

three girls are nine, seven, and two. "Having a home-based business has given us the opportunity

to balance family and career in the best possible way," says Hull, who adds, "We want to help

others who are trying to do the same thing."

*For more information on <u>Moneymaking Moms: How Work at Home Can Work for You</u> con-
tact Caroline Hull or Tanya Wallace at 703/555-1234.*

- End -

End text with
"-End-", or "###", or "-30-"

Finish with a quote

- Put the most important information immediately after the headline in the first paragraph. Remember, you'll be lucky if more than the first few lines are read, so you have to make it compelling.

- Try to fit your release onto one page, but if you have to use a second page, make sure that you identify the second page as page 2 of two and head it up with the same heading, or part of it, as the first page. Put "more" at the bottom of the first page.

- Finish release off with "# # #" or "END."

- Include at least one quote, if possible, to personalize the release.

- Remember, the easier you make the editor's job, the more likely it is that he or she will put a writer on the story.

Building a Media Mail List

Whenever you send out a press release, always send it to a specific contact within the news organization. Don't just send it to the editor at the *ABC Journal,* because it will probably get lost in the shuffle. Call ahead of time to find out which department your announcement is most suited for and then ask for a name and title of an appropriate contact. Add the name to your media mailing list. If you read an article in a newspaper or magazine or even see a feature on television that relates to your work, add the name of the reporters involved to your list, too. If they were sufficiently interested in the topic to report on it once, they may be interested in pursuing it again.

Your rule of thumb should be: Whatever your potential customers read, watch, or listen to is where you want to be featured. Build a list of media contacts from newspapers, trade publications, magazines, local TV, cable, and radio stations, and update the list every six months or so to make sure that your contacts haven't moved on somewhere else. If so, get the name of the new jobholder and make the change to your media list. If possible, find out where your original contact has moved and add that to your list, too!

It is possible to get media coverage, and there is a huge media market out there. Interesting stories and features are always in

What Publicity Can Do for Your Business

Both Tanya and Caroline have benefited from the publicity generated by press releases they mailed. Tanya's company Toddlin' Time was featured on several local cable broadcasts and publicized in three national-franchise magazines after she did a mass mailing to seventy-five publications a few years ago. The company has consistently appeared in *Entrepreneur* magazine's "Annual Franchise 500" since, and she sold five more franchises as a direct result of leads generated by this publicity.

Caroline's frequent news releases about mothers and home-based business have led to appearances on several national network and cable TV shows, and on radio and to numerous references in both national and local newspapers and magazines. Most of it resulted in a nicely manageable surge in subscribers to her newsletter, *ConneXions*, and cemented her reputation as an advocate and "expert" in the field of home-based business and alternative work options.

Make sure you are prepared for the response favorable publicity can generate for your business. If your business telephone number is publicized, you may get more calls than you can handle. If your business address is used, make sure you can afford the postage to send information to people who write to you. And if you sell a product, make sure you have sufficient inventory on hand to meet the potential increase in demand!

demand, particularly for media that operate on a daily basis. They have a lot of space to fill each week! It may take a while before you get anywhere with this strategy but don't give up. Set yourself a target of issuing a quarterly news release to your media list and try to come up with a slightly different "hook" each time. Don't "bug" your contacts but be helpful and courteous if they call you, if only to use you as a resource and quote your opinion in a related feature, although the main focus isn't on you. Always send a note of appreciation to the reporter when you have received favorable publicity. Keep your press clippings in a file or have clean copies made that include the masthead of the publication and the date. Ask radio or TV producers if they will make a cassette or videotape available to you, even if you have to pay a small fee.

Here are some of the types of publications you may want to approach about media coverage for your business:

- Local and community newspapers.
- National magazines and periodicals that relate to the type of business you run. If your home business is very unique, publications about home-based businesses may be interested in profiling you.
- National newsletters that cover your trade.
- News magazines on television.
- Your local news channels. Often the afternoon and early-evening broadcasts include some human-interest segments.

So get busy on the phone or on your computer and let the media know you're out there. Remember, be excited about your business: Enthusiasm is contagious, and they just might catch it!

Networking

We covered networking in detail in Phase II as a way to stay connected to the world outside your home-office door. But you should also regard networking actively as a wonderful way to market your business and make contacts to expand your business network. Remind yourself of the benefits by going back to pages 142–52 and make sure you include some active networking in your marketing bag of tricks.

Public Speaking

You are a self-proclaimed entrepreneur, so don't be surprised when people are interested in what you have to say. In fact, use your

---

BITS 'N BYTES PRESENTS......

Upgrade or Buy New?
What's a Computer User to Do?

When?   Monday, June 18, 1996

What time?   7:00 p.m. - 9:30 p.m.

Where?   Smalltown Community Center
                   123 Oak Lane, Smalltown

How much?   FREE....FREE....FREE....FREE!!!!!

Bring your upgrade questions with you and come ready to learn about the latest technological developments in the computer world!

R.S.V.P   703-555-1234

REFRESHMENTS WILL BE SERVED

---

knowledge and skill as a marketing tool and speak up! You may even develop a second career for yourself!

By making yourself available for public speaking, even if you do it for free, you are letting the public know about you and your business. You can contact local groups to let them know you are available to speak to their membership—networking organizations, moms' clubs, and professional and trade groups, for example.

Or you may wish to organize your own seminar and publicize it. You choose the topic (make sure you know what you're talking about!) and the place, notify the press, mail postcards (like the one above) announcing your lecture, and if funds allow, advertise the event in the local paper. If you charge a fee, make sure it is nominal but still covers most, if not all, of your expenses to hold the event. Room rental, advertising, refreshments, and handout material can all add up. Establish a reservations policy so that you won't be caught off guard by an especially large (or small) turnout.

Select an appropriate venue for the topic you are addressing. If you are an interior decorator, then lining up a presentation at the local Elks lodge on "Fraternity Night" doesn't make much sense. But the local wallpaper and designer-fabric store might be just the place to hold an informal lecture on the dos and don'ts of decorating a home.

Note: If funds are especially tight, your local library or community center may be able to offer you a room either free or for a very small charge.

Pointers on Public Speaking

Public speaking can be intimidating unless you have experience. You'll probably experience a few butterflies the first time you step up to the podium, but the more you do it, the easier it becomes. Delivering a good speech isn't difficult, but there are some pointers and techniques that will enhance your presentation.

- *Plan what you are going to say and don't try and "wing it."* There's nothing worse than listening to someone "um" and "ah" through a rambling talk. Prepare yourself adequately and bring notes you can refer to, as necessary.

- *Deliver.* Be aware of what your audience is expecting from you and make sure you can deliver it. Presumably, you are there because of your own experience, but if necessary, do some background research to back up what you are saying.

- *Use humor.* Don't be afraid to use humor in your talks; it can be an effective icebreaker at the beginning of your presentation and instantly endear you to your audience.

- *Use visual aids if appropriate.* If you are giving an educational talk, it might be helpful to prepare some visual aids—flip chart, slide presentation, photographic "before and afters," or even just a marker board. This helps keep the audience's attention focused and gives your presentation a professional feel.

- *Bring handouts.* It's always helpful to supplement a talk or seminar with printed material that reinforces the subject covered and/or adds more information. Consider bringing handouts for your attendees, especially if you have amassed useful resource information pertinent to your topic. Also make sure you have plenty of business cards and brochures on hand.

■ *Dress the part.* You need to dress appropriately for your audience. If you are speaking to a roomful of company executives, your dress should be relatively formal. But if your audience is mainly moms, a more casual approach will enable them to relate to you better.

■ *Practice your delivery.* Whatever you do, don't just read a sheaf of notes. Study your speech and be ready to talk with only an occasional glance at your notes. Make frequent eye contact with the audience all around the room, not just in one small section. Move around rather than standing stiffly behind the lectern. Be expressive and smile often.

■ *Be prepared for audience questions.* Find out in advance if there will be time for a Q & A session after your talk, and if you are interrupted during your speech, assure the audience there will be time for questions later.

■ *Practice and improve.* Join a public speaking organization such as Toastmasters International. Weekly meetings provide a framework for members to practice and improve public-speaking skills in a supportive environment.

Teaching a Course or Workshop

A related activity is teaching a course or workshop through your local community center or college. In this case, generally the campus or community facility will promote and market the course. All you have to do is show up prepared to teach on the day your class is scheduled! Contact your local community centers and college campuses and offer to teach a course in your specialty. They have been known to create new courses if the ideas are good and the instructor is knowledgeable. Give it a try!

Writing an Article

One of the by-products of running a business is to become more adept at communicating through the written word. Coupled with the expertise you have developed in your field, you have the basis for an interesting article on some aspect of your business or lifestyle. Magazines, periodicals, and newsletters are always on the lookout for a well-written, thoughtful piece that is informative and entertaining at the same time.

If you have an idea, write it down. If you are a good writer, submit the article to a magazine or other publication you regularly read and that you feel may be interested in your topic. If you have the background knowledge but feel your writing is shaky, team up with a friend or contact who does write well and offer to include her name on the byline with yours.

Before you venture off to your computer to write your masterpiece, however, make a quick call to the publications you intend to approach with your work. Ask them for a copy of their writer's guidelines or other instructions on how they want articles to be submitted. They might want a query letter from you first rather than receiving the entire submission.

Getting published firmly establishes your credentials and enhances your business reputation. Reprints of your published article(s) can accompany press releases and marketing materials, impressing both media and prospects; keep them in a separate file so that you can access them at a moment's notice. Make sure you supply the publication with a brief bio for the byline that includes both your name and the name of your business. If you are to be published in a national publication, make sure they also include your city and state, too, so that readers can locate you if desired.

Stay in touch with the editor or publisher who accepted your article. They will be good contacts for future publishing efforts.

A Personal Glimpse Loraine Goodenough knows all about innovative marketing. She's become a seasoned veteran during her nine years in business! Loraine admits that when she first started

Getting the Most Out of Your Marketing Dollar

- Watch for information on upcoming networking functions in newspapers and other publications. Attend as many as you can and bring as much marketing material with you as possible. If the press is present introduce yourself and make sure they get some of your marketing literature, too; it just might be your ticket to some of that free publicity we've talked about.

- Stay in touch with the media. Send out regular press releases about your business or upcoming events you are sponsoring. The trick is to try—and often. It may take months before your company is contacted, but the publicity payoff is worth waiting for.

- Make yourself available for public speaking, participation in charitable events, and community celebrations. You'll keep your name in the public eye and establish a reputation as a generous, community-oriented business.

- Always analyze what your favorite businesses do to keep you as a customer; it may be a technique you can use yourself to attract and retain a loyal client base.

- Carry your business cards with you wherever you go and hand them out freely. They are the cheapest marketing tool around.

- Adopt a street. Many local communities encourage local businesses to "adopt" a street which they agree to help keep free from debris and litter. In return, the business name appears on an Adopt-a-Street road sign. Contact your local government office to see how you can participate in this type of program. Choose a street that is relatively low maintenance yet well traveled so that your trash pickup is kept to a minimum, but your name exposure is maximized.

Rainy Day Communications, she was "relatively clueless" about marketing, but she has come a long way since then.

Loraine now markets her company through a variety of shoestring techniques, and her business has grown and flourished as a result. Here are some of the marketing tools that have helped her business grow.

- *Sending a newsletter.* Loraine teamed up with two other businesses to write and publish a newsletter that they send to their combined mailing lists. "The three of us got together and agreed that we are after the same market; why not make a joint effort? It splits the costs; we get a better product and the benefit of the three combined mailing lists for a larger distribution."

- *Volunteering her time—selectively.* As an admitted "recovering volunteer," Loraine has set ground rules about who and what she donates her time to. "It [volunteering] should make me feel good, but it should also *benefit the business* somehow. For example, at my daughter's class at school, I don't have time to be the room parent, but I did volunteer to put together the class directory, which gives me credit on the cover for doing so."

- *Networking everywhere!* "I take business cards to the pool! Networking got me most of my clients in the early days of my business and continues to do so. Why? Because they recognize me and know how to reach me. It establishes my credibility as they see the samples of my work that I bring to each event. Plus, I get free exposure every time my name is mentioned in the member newsletters—and I try to get my name in every issue!"

- *Sending personal note cards.* "People remember that personal touch. When I write a personal note, I always make sure that I reference something I can remember from the last time we met. It lets them know that I remember who they are, and it never sounds like I'm sending them a form letter."

- *Teaching workshops.* Loraine frequently teaches a county-sponsored workshop on networking techniques and has recently begun offering seminars with her newsletter partners. "It gives me credibility, and besides, I like the applause!"

Loraine's innovative marketing enabled her to relocate her home office from a cramped corner of the kitchen to her newly remodeled basement last year. The only downside of that, says Loraine, is the extra flight of stairs, which "doubled my commute time!"

Charitable Activities

It may be your community that keeps you in business, and if so, you need to give a little something back. It's a generous way of saying thank you while establishing your reputation as a community-oriented business. There are many ways of helping your community. Here are some ideas:

Adopt a family for the holidays. Each Christmas there are too many toys left on the shelves and far too many children with nothing to open. You can help! Contact the local homeless shelter or social-services office in your area. Ask if you can adopt a family or, if your budget allows, more than one. They will usually be able to provide you with a list of family members, their ages, and their wish list for Christmas. If possible, get your clients involved. Encourage them to adopt a family, too, and then organize it for them.

Get involved in a toy drive for the holidays. Again, involve your clients in helping with a toy drive to benefit the needy in your community. Send out press releases stating that you are organizing a drive and that your business will be the drop-off center. Your local social-services office will be only too happy to distribute the toys you collect.

Do a school fund-raiser or auction. Approach local preschools and grade schools and offer to do a fund-raiser or auction for them. You might want to round up a few other businesses to participate and agree on a percentage of profits to donate to the school. If organizing it yourself isn't a possibility, watch out for events you can contribute to.

Sponsor a sports team. Youth sports teams are so important and usually run by parents generously volunteering their time to organize and coach them. Even if you don't have time to get involved in that way, you could offer to sponsor a team. It's generally a very inexpensive way to make a contribution, and your business name will be worn proudly on all those little chests!

Put together a charitable carnival. These can be organized through combined community efforts. Organize a carnival to take place on a Saturday. Have plenty of games, food, and other attractions on hand and ask area businesses for donations in time, money, and supplies for the event. The carnival should be open to the public for a donation of one new item for needy children, such as socks, diapers, underwear, clothing, and winter wear. Publicize it by sending press releases to the media (at least six weeks before the event) and by posting fliers in grocery stores, libraries, community centers, and area businesses. As it is a not-for-profit community event, the media and many businesses will be prepared to help get the word out. If a full-blown carnival is out of the question, consider a puppet show, food festival, or block party instead. As the sponsor and organizer of the event, your business will benefit favorably from the publicity, too.

Donate park equipment. If it has been an especially good year, ask your local government if you can donate a piece of equipment to the local park. Most will snap up the opportunity to replace aging benches, trash containers, and playground equipment; install more lights for safety or improve landscaping with a donation of trees and flowers. Once again, don't be shy about contacting the media to let them know of your company's generous donation.

Organize a clean-up. You just might be surprised at the number of people ready and willing to help! Choose a Saturday and start early. Organize a meeting place and assign work areas. Have at least two adults in each group you send out and avoid highways or busy streets that could be dangerous. Provide large plastic bags and send them on their way. Invite the press to cover the event and announce it ahead of time. Consider having T-shirts or sweatshirts made that display your company name as sponsor of "Smalltown Cleanup Day." If you do get pictorial coverage, your business name will be prominently displayed for all to see!

Don't forget, any expenses that your business incurs in setting up these special events or assisting the needy are tax-deductible, so keep careful records. All of these suggestions could benefit your local community, and you'll get kudos for being sponsor and organizer. You'll also make new contacts that can benefit your business and feel the satisfaction of giving something back to the community that supports you.

Remembering the Personal Touch

It's hard to ignore the fact that we live in an increasingly impersonal world in which technology dominates even the most mundane daily tasks. We are called by and then put on hold by computers; we dial a number, only to reach an automated announcement that emotionlessly lists our options; we pay our bills and manage our money without ever having to talk to another human being, and we can even purchase fresh-cut flowers through a vending machine! Whatever happened to the human touch? Our children are growing up in a world in which the term "personal service" has all but disappeared.

But human beings as a species are programmed to interact and communicate. Although sometimes it's convenient to hurry through an automated transaction, most of us benefit from regular, positive interactions with other individuals. You can capitalize on this in your business dealings by making client relations a top priority. You will impress your customers in a way no automation-dependent corporation can.

It isn't hard to do or even that time-consuming. For example, contact a client after you've finished a job to make sure that you met expectations. It will only take a few minutes, but the positive impact of your actions will last much longer. Other personal touches could include making courtesy calls to clients and letting them know when you are having a special on a favorite product; sending a handwritten note saying, "Thank you for your business"; remembering your loyal customers with a personalized Christmas or Hanukkah card. They are all ways to show your clients that they are important to you and you value their business.

Take care of your clients and they will return again and again. The mere fact that you make the effort to deal with them on a very personal level puts you way ahead of competitors who don't.

Maintaining a Positive Business Image

Image—it's how the public perceives you. If the impression you leave with your clients is favorable, it will be another marketing tool working for you. But if your clients are "underwhelmed" with your presence, no amount of marketing will bring you the repeat business that successful companies thrive on.

Here's our set of "rules" for leaving a positive impression every time:

- *Be prompt.* If you schedule a meeting for 1:00 P.M. *make sure you are there by 1:00 P.M.!* If you tend to run late, schedule the meeting in your planner for 12:30 P.M. and allow yourself an extra half hour. You can always find a coffee shop and prepare yourself for the meeting while you wait.

- *Show your gratitude.* Anyone who has been at all instrumental in helping your business grow deserves your heartfelt thanks. Whether it's a satisfied client who referred a friend or a printer who made sure your order was rushed through to meet a deadline, let them know how much you appreciate their help.

- *Maintain an energetic and positive attitude about your business,* at least when you're in public! If you're having trouble feeling upbeat, go back to Phase II and reread our sections on motivation and goal setting.

- *Think about your "paper" image, too.* Much of your image is your printed material; sometimes that's *all* people see. We can't stress enough that even if you have very little start-up cash, you should invest in good, clean, professional stationery. It's better to have just business cards and a letterhead that look good than a whole range of crummy-looking paper.

- *Don't leave customers or prospects hanging.* If you are leaving town for any reason (including family vacations) check your messages on a regular basis. Return important calls from clients and resolve any problems immediately. If necessary, let them know that you are not in town but you will address the situation as soon as you return to the office. Remember, your happy clients are the ones that bring referrals your way.

- *Be prepared to admit you're wrong.* If you know you've made a mistake, assure the client that you will do everything in your power to rectify the situation. Simply admitting that you were wrong earns you bonus points with most clients, who will respect you for your honesty.

- *Toot your own horn.* Since you are the public-relations department for your business, be prepared to talk it up! Keep friends, family, business associates, and clients aware of your progress and stay excited and passionate about what you are doing. Your enthusiasm will be contagious!

- *Keep your life in perspective.* Remember why you opted to work at home in the first place—because you wanted to be there for your children. Sometimes it's easy to lose sight of priorities when you're really busy or you just want to get something finished before dinnertime. But you and the family will all be happier if everyone knows that they are your priority.

- *Don't forget the importance of time management.* When you feel yourself becoming overwhelmed and out of sorts because your schedule is just too hectic, step back and reevaluate your workload. Reread our section on time management and allocate at least one half-hour to one hour each day for planning your time.

- *Treat every day as a new one.* You will experience bad days as a business owner and mother. A disgruntled client, an uncooperative two-year-old, a dispute over a bill or an order—you'll no doubt be confronted with all three. And if the stars are lining up just right, they will all occur on the same day! Take a deep breath and face each problem in turn. The day will end, the customer disputes will be solved, the two-year-old will finally fall asleep, and you will know that tomorrow is another day. It is all part of the wonderful, crazy world of the home-based working mom. Pat yourself on the back;

only the brave ones tread where you stand! You should be proud, even on the most challenging of days.

- *Take an image inventory of your business.* Ask yourself how you are doing. Have you lost clients because of careless mistakes or outrageous pricing? Is the phone ringing regularly? Are you getting lots of repeat business and client referrals? If not, analyze where your weaknesses lie and do something about them.

Maintaining a positive image doesn't actually cost you anything except some time and effort, but the payback to you will be worth every second. It's another marketing tool that will help you grow.

The "Five-Tool" Rule

You've probably noticed that you are more likely to try a new product if you see or read about it more than once and in a few different places. For example, you might receive a promotional mailer introducing a new baby product which you read with interest at the time but then quickly forgot. However, if you are continually exposed to that product by seeing ads for it, read a brief article about it in a parenting magazine, and *then* see a discount coupon for it at the toy store, you are much more likely to go ahead and purchase it.

The basic concept behind such a multipronged approach is to maximize the number of times potential customers see the same information; it's a technique large corporations use all the time, and even on a limited budget, you can, too. The point is that the more we are exposed to information about a particular product or service, the more likely we are to clip the ad or put the coupon in our wallet and act on it. So, when planning a marketing campaign, companies will always use several different marketing techniques. They call this the "marketing mix."

We call it the five-tool rule. That is, aiming to have five marketing tools working for you at any given time. Practicing this rule will increase your exposure, and when one tool isn't working for you on a particular day, another will.

For example, Kerry is a landscape architect who is trying to establish her business, Kerry Landscapes, in town. Her objective is to double her client base during the busy spring and summer seasons. Following the five-tool rule, she employs five different marketing tools over the course of several weeks in order to meet her goal:

1. She contracts with a coupon cooperative for a coupon mailing to residences offering a discount on an initial consultation.
2. She places a series of small display ads in the "Homes" section of the local newspaper.
3. She offers monthly talks in cooperation with local garden stores and sends out press releases to publicize them.
4. She attends monthly networking meetings of her local home-based business group and the chamber of commerce.
5. She donates her time to design a garden for a local nursery, and in return the store erects a placard next to the display, saying, Designed by Kerry Landscapes.

With all those tools working for her, it will be hard for her potential prospects to *avoid* exposure to her business! Coordinating a marketing effort like this will take a bit of planning but will work much better than implementing one tool at a time.

We recommend that you review your marketing efforts regularly and check how many tools you have actively working for you. It might be time to get another tool out of your kit!

Marketing is the lifeline of your business. Look at it this way—if you don't nourish your children, they won't grow healthy and strong. Think of marketing as the fuel your business needs to grow and flourish. So get busy keeping your business alive and well! *Market!*

16

Troubleshooting

No matter how good your product, service, and overall business tactics may be, you're going to run into a difficult situation sooner or later. Whether it's a dissatisfied client, a misprint in your expensive advertisement, an order that got lost en route, or a computer that crashes on you at a crucial moment, you can count on being confronted with problems of some sort as your business grows.

We hope that you won't find yourself in a troubleshooting mode very often, but when you do, your first concern must be your customers. Even if the problem wasn't directly caused by you, you still have to find a way to meet your business obligations and fulfill your commitments. The first time something goes badly wrong is when you are most likely to panic. But you don't have to! If you can anticipate general problems you are likely to run into, you can prepare yourself with a damage-control plan and implement it fast when trouble shows up!

When It's Not Your Fault

It's natural to kick yourself when you do something stupid or make a mistake, but it feels even worse when someone else made the mistake but *you* have to pick up the pieces.

Because your business doesn't operate in a vacuum and you are dependent on others, someone else's problem can very easily become yours. Whether you rely on a shipping service to mail packages, hire subcontractors to work on your larger projects, or depend on a supplier to keep your inventory stocked, you are vulnerable if they run into trouble.

But the fact remains that as a business owner you are accountable to your customers *whether or not you caused the problem.* If your customers are going to be negatively affected in any way, you must notify them promptly and let them know what you are doing to rectify the situation. You must take control of the situation and actively try to resolve it or at least repair the damage that has been caused. This isn't the time to bury your head in the sand and hope things work out or simply throw up your hands in despair because you weren't to blame. You owe it to your customers to take accountability (if not responsibility) and act quickly and diligently to prevent a problem situation from blowing up into a full-scale disaster.

For example, Julia was a photojournalist who decided to stay home and open a portrait studio in her basement after the birth of her first child. Rather than develop the film herself, she sent it to an out-of-state developing service for processing. Each day she mailed the rolls of film she had used, which were then returned to her as proofs within five business days.

The arrangement was cost-effective and worked well for Julia until one fateful day when she realized that she was missing the proofs from one day's work. On checking with the developing service, she was told that they had no record of receiving the film. Apparently, her package had gone astray in the mail.

Julia's first reaction was to panic. She had not only lost an entire day's work and several rolls of expensive film, but the three clients involved were all new to her studio and she wasn't happy about facing them with the bad news. She knew she had to come up with a creative solution to minimize the damage and make the best of a bad situation.

The first step in her damage-control plan was to contact her clients (before they called *her*, looking for their proofs) and let them know what had happened. She gave a brief explanation of the problem, apologized profusely, and assured them that she would do whatever she could to rectify the situation. She then offered each client the following:

- A repeat session (at no charge, obviously) at her studio or, if more convenient, at the client's home.
- A free eight-by-ten photograph.
- A 20 percent discount coupon to use in a future session.

She hoped that by offering an incentive that wouldn't cost her too much to implement but was really too good to turn down, she could keep her customers' business and their goodwill. Although her clients were initially irritated at having to repeat the photo sessions, all three returned and were ultimately delighted with their finished photographs.

Because Julia handled things promptly and creatively, she was able to turn the situation around. All three clients continued to use her services and refer her to their friends. Julia learned from the experience that she could handle a difficult situation without it ruining her business and became more confident as a result. She also realized that perhaps it was time to review her shipping policy and switched to a company that tracked all its packages, although it would cost a little more. She adjusted her fees to cover the increased overhead.

Julia handled the situation well, and luckily her clients were prepared to go along with the way she offered to make amends. It would be nice if business problems could always be resolved so well! But sometimes whatever you do, however hard you try, they just can't. What do you do when despite your best efforts, your client is still dissatisfied and openly grumbling about your product or service?

The Disgruntled Client

Customers can become disgruntled for a variety of reasons. They might just be having a bad day, or their expectations of you may not have been realistic, or they may have a justifiable complaint about the way you have handled something. Our advice? Do whatever it takes (within reason!) to turn the situation around and make the customer happy, because a disgruntled client can be really bad for your business. Here are some tips:

▪ *Listen.* Don't interrupt a customer who is venting. Listen intently until he or she has finished explaining the problem. Being listened to can have a calming effect on even the most irate individuals.

▪ *Don't go on the defensive.* You don't have to admit liability or that you have done anything wrong, but you can sympathize with the client and promise to look into the problem. If you get defensive, you are inviting a more heated response, and the situation could easily get out of hand.

▪ *Take time to consider the situation and your options for resolving it.* Even if your customer is extremely upset, don't be tempted to throw an immediate decision at him. Give yourself and the client time to step back from the situation and calm down.

▪ *Be honest.* Don't try to lie your way out of a problem. Responding to an angry customer with an obvious lie is like offering a red rag to a bull. You'll aggravate the situation and lose your credibility along with any hope of resolving things.

▪ *Refer back to your contract.* Sometimes a client forgets what was originally agreed to and can harangue you for something that was never in the contract to begin with! Point this out politely but firmly and provide another copy of the signed contract with the pertinent clause(s) highlighted.

▪ *Remember the bottom line:* An unhappy customer is like a loose cannon and can do your business a lot of harm. Even if you feel that the customer is in the wrong, do what you can to salvage the situation and chalk it up to experience.

The Problem Client

We've all heard the adage the customer is always right, but there are times when you know the customer is just downright *wrong!* Every business owner dreads having to deal with the client who is nothing but a problem from start to finish. Unlike a disgruntled client who may have a legitimate gripe, the problem client doesn't pay his bills on time, his checks bounce when you finally get them, or his behavior in some other way is having a negative impact on your business. What do you do?

• *"Fire" your client.* It may sound silly, but if you have consistently experienced problems with a customer, it's probably starting to cost you money to service the account, and you need to offload the burden. Politely and professionally terminate the relationship, even if you have to take a loss on the project.

• *Stand your ground.* Don't be intimidated by someone if you know you are absolutely in the right. There's a time to be accommodating and a time to stand your ground. You don't have to be a pushover.

• *Consider legal action.* If all else fails, be prepared to take legal action to recover money that is owed you, especially if there is a significant sum involved. You don't necessarily have to hire an attorney and prepare to do battle; cases like this can often be handled in small-claims courts. But, as a plaintiff, the burden of proof will be on you, so make sure you have a good case and the documentation to back you up.

• *Get a signed receipt.* Always ask your customers to sign an invoice or delivery receipt stating that they have received (and are satisfied with) the product or service you provided.

• *Learn from the experience!* Look for "warning signs" when talking to prospective clients. Those that want to nickel-and-dime you to death, rewrite your contract, or balk at paying your standard deposit may be more trouble than they are worth.

A Personal Glimpse   Lisa Martin's business is only two years old, but she already counts Mobil, Macworld, Phillips 66, and several large trade associations among her clients. Lisa, a mother of two, formed the company in 1995, pulling together a team of independent, creative specialists who would provide an extensive array of strategic marketing and creative services under the auspices of a single organization, LeapFrog Solutions.

LeapFrog Solutions offers website design, trade-show planning, CD-ROM design and development, video production, copywriting/ design of brochures, and other marketing pieces among its services. The business operates as a "virtual company." Each of the nine team members works as an independent contractor out of his or her own office, although to their clients they appear to be an integral unit. Lisa brings in the business and then becomes the project manager and liaison on each account, coordinating the various members of the team and aspects of the job.

With annual billings of more than $250,000, LeapFrog has more than met initial projections and expectations during its short time in business. Lisa's policy from the outset has been to get a 50 percent deposit from her clients before the team starts work. Not only does this help defray LeapFrog's ongoing costs, but she also hoped that a sizable up-front monetary commitment would help weed out potential problem clients and those that couldn't or wouldn't pay. Unfortunately, it wasn't enough to avoid problems with one of her early clients.

Lisa admits to being "networked to the hilt," and the client in question, like many of Lisa's accounts, was a referral from one of her many networking contacts. Although Lisa sensed that there were money problems, her fledgling business was only weeks old and "hungry for business," so she took on the account. The client paid the initial deposit with no objections, but it was all downhill from there on.

Lisa, per her normal practice, priced the job based on initial discussions and agreements with the client. She knew that the rates she quoted were fair and competitive; her 'virtual company' setup minimized her overhead, and her pricing reflected those savings.

But she hadn't allowed for the constant changes and deviations from the original plan the client demanded, and he didn't want to accept the fact that he would be charged extra. As if this weren't enough, the foreign owner evidently hailed from a culture that regarded women as second-class citizens, or at least as unacceptable in the business world. Lisa's meetings with him were made arduous by his refusal to respond to her directly. Instead, he would only direct his answers to Lisa's male colleague, even though she was the main contact and asked all the questions! Despite this additional complication, Lisa persevered and made the best of the awkward situation.

When the project was completed and delivered, Lisa invoiced the client for the remaining balance, which amounted to several thousand dollars. It quickly became apparent that despite constant reminders initially, followed by subsequent demands, payment was not forthcoming. Lisa finally confronted her main contact at the firm, who confessed that *she* hadn't even been paid her salary for three months. In fact, things were *so* bad, she admitted, that she had actually taken the drastic step of using her own personal credit card to pay one of LeapFrog's invoices and was hoping to get reimbursed via expenses.

Lisa's instincts told her that she had probably already wasted enough time trying to recover the money owed her, particularly in light of the employee's predicament. But then the client approached her to work on another rush project, and Lisa saw it as an opportunity to finally get paid for the work done earlier. She took on the job, provided he paid the long-overdue bill and agreed to pay for any future work at the time of delivery.

Unfortunately, the problems didn't end there. Lisa found that the team was still putting in much more work than anticipated because, as before, the client kept changing things. The outstanding balance was never completely cleared, so eventually Lisa felt she had no choice but to walk away from the client—and from the money he owed her. It just wasn't worth the time and annoyance anymore.

But a surprise turn of events made her reconsider her decision. She received a call from her former contact (now also a former employee!), who was suing the company for six months of unpaid salary. She urged Lisa to sue for the money that she was owed, too. Although Lisa had considered suing before, after weighing the pros and cons, she decided that it would cost less in time, stress, and legal fees to write the whole episode off and just chalk it up to experience. But her outrage at the way this ethically challenged client handled not only vendors but his own staff forced her hand, and she decided to sue after all.

Lisa still hopes that she might be able to settle the case without going to court. If the case does end up in litigation, she is not optimistic about her chances of ever getting paid, even if she should win. But the situation has become as much a matter of principle after so long. At least a win for her would mean a judgment entered against the company that has caused so much trouble and hasn't lived up to its obligations.

Lisa has invested valuable time and energy on the problems caused by one difficult customer, but she chooses to categorize the ordeal as a learning experience—a hands-on lesson on the sometimes harsh reality of business ownership. Regardless of the outcome, things are going well at LeapFrog, and Lisa hasn't let this isolated situation bog her down. She is too busy building a successful, profitable business! She plans to double revenues in her next fiscal year and is revamping her business plan to reflect that goal. It takes more than one difficult customer to quash a true entrepreneur!

17

Growing Pains

Strangely enough, one of the toughest parts of being a moneymaking mom is pacing the growth of your business. A business that grows too fast too soon can create as many problems for a home-based mom as a business that languishes and doesn't go anywhere.

Let's face it, most of us have chosen to work from home in an effort to simplify our lives and spend more time with family. There's no doubt that a thriving business is a greedy competitor for attention, and if you're not careful, it can eat up all that good quality time you found by coming home in the first place.

But you may arrive at a point where you have to make a decision to grow—or not. This often requires some soul-searching, as a larger business generally means larger problems and a more complicated situation. The first threshold is usually reached when you realize that it's time to hire an assistant to help with the workload or to free you up to do more marketing. Becoming an "employer" puts you in a whole different league as a business owner and brings with it different responsibilities and obligations. It can take time before a new employee is really functional, and until then, you will probably find your workload even larger as you spend time on training the new hire. When you're used to doing everything yourself, it can be frustrating to delegate tasks you know you could do in half the time!

If your company continues to grow and flourish, at some point you will reach the second major threshold—the decision to remain home-based or move your operation to outside office space. As a home-based business grows, it tends to take over more and more of your home's living space and simply becomes too invasive to tolerate. This is when you have to take a long, hard look at where you are in your personal life and whether you feel comfortable taking this serious step. If not, your alternative would probably be to scale back and restore the business to a more manageable level—not an easy task.

Kathy Benson faced these issues—and more—as her business, Office Remedies, Inc., has grown from the one-woman organization she started in 1988. Here's her story:

Kathy realized shortly after the birth of her first child that a full-time job and motherhood wasn't the right mix for her. She felt that she was "doing a lot for a little," and it was keeping her away from her baby. Although she couldn't afford to give up her income, Kathy began to think of ways she could bring her work home, and the business idea she came up with was based on two premises. First, her years of experience in administrative roles led Kathy to believe that much of the work done in offices could be handled just as efficiently off-site. Second, she knew that there had to be scores of other moms like her who were searching for a way to stay home with their children but have an opportunity to make money at the same time.

So she started Office Remedies, Inc., offering off-site data-entry services to local corporations. For the first couple of years, Kathy was the lone "employee," working nights and weekends to find work and fulfill contracts while she continued her full-time job during the day. As the jobs began to flow in, she approached other "moms at home" to work as independent contractors, and the operation began to grow.

Her efforts paid off, and two years later Kathy was able to leave her job and devote her energies to Office Remedies, which she ran from her basement. At this point Kathy had been joined part-time by her business partner, Sue, and Kathy began marketing in earnest knowing she could find enough moms who would seize the opportunity to make money at home. It was an ideal situation—plenty of business, plenty of help, but none of the complications of a large staff or any problems with space!

However, as Office Remedies was building its customer base, American companies were downsizing and frequently replacing employees with subcontractors to save money. As a result, the IRS had begun to scrutinize contract versus employee situations and tighten regulations governing employee status. After consulting with her accountant and attorney, Kathy realized that she needed to approach the IRS and ask them for a ruling on her organization, as she was a relatively unique case. The IRS response was to classify Kathy's workers as part-time employees rather than independent subcontractors. Suddenly, Kathy was an *employer* with *twenty* employees! Life had become a little more complicated.

Ironically though, the impact of this IRS ruling had a positive effect on Kathy's business and ultimately led to several growth-related changes in the way she ran the business. In fact, it was like the first domino had fallen, and each subsequent domino that fell led to more changes!

The first big change was in how they managed the payroll. Because her workers were now employees, Kathy now had various tax and withholding obligations to consider, so she contracted Automatic Data Processing (ADP) to handle the increasingly complex payroll that had been done in-house to that point. Now her employees received a monthly paycheck rather than waiting to get paid after the client had remitted payment for the project. But this meant that Kathy had to negotiate a line of credit with the bank to enable her to manage cash flow and cover the monthly salary commitment. This in turn forced her to pay more attention to her profit and bottom line—issues she hadn't paid as much attention to until then. Despite the stress involved in all these transitions, Kathy admits that the net effect was actually to make her more "businesslike" about her business.

As business continued to grow steadily over the next year or two, Kathy was fast approaching her second major decision—whether she should move the business out of her home. By now the number of moms employed part-time had swelled to forty-seven, and they also had a part-time salesperson and two part-time programmers. Kathy, Sue, and an office manager all worked full-time. Kathy's basement was getting pretty crowded! The environment had become chaotic. Between the ringing phones, the constant courier arrivals, and the dog barking, Kathy and Sue had to face the fact that it was no longer feasible to remain a home-based operation. Plus, increasingly they were winning jobs that involved sensitive material that had to be dealt with at the main office location. If things were to continue, they had to relocate.

So they were faced with a decision. Should they keep growing and move, or should they scale back the business and stay home-based? The decision was complicated by Kathy's absolute commitment to support the women who worked for her; some had been with her since the beginning of her business. If Office Remedies was to continue to provide employment for these moms, it couldn't take a backward step. The solution seemed clear. They began to look for office space.

But not just any office space! Kathy was determined to wait until the right location materialized. First, it had to be at ground-floor level, with easy, convenient access. Kathy was worried that her moms wouldn't be able to negotiate an elevator or stairs, plus the boxes of paper they were delivering or picking up, plus any little ones they had in tow. She was also adamant that their parking spaces be right outside the office door—again to facilitate pickups and drop-offs without having to disturb sleeping babies. Finally, it had to be nearby so that Kathy could get home within minutes.

It took a couple of months of looking, but finally they found the "perfect space"—twenty-two hundred square feet of ground-floor accommodation less than ten minutes from Kathy's house, with parking right outside, and that met all her requirements for convenient access.

The move was made. Now they had to budget for a monthly lease payment and other expenses as well as furnish and equip the office.

It was a big step—and a serious transition. But it was a move Kathy was ready to make. Her two children were now ten and seven years old and at school during the day. She had deliberately paced the company's growth to coincide with her children's increasing independence. She couldn't and *wouldn't* have moved to an office space when they were younger. In fact, she acknowledges that Office Remedies would probably have been "a lot further on now" if she had let it run its course.

What challenges now face Kathy? Number one is the ongoing struggle to balance work and family; it's never easy to do when you are running a business, but a little tougher when your business has grown beyond one or two employees. Kathy now goes to the office at 9:00 A.M., after the children leave for school, and returns by 4:00 P.M., when they get home. She has kept an office in the basement, where she usually puts in another two hours or so while the children are doing their homework or after they have gone to bed. Her other most pressing challenge is looking ahead and coming up with ideas to diversify and keep up with the rapid technological changes in her industry.

But at the end of the day Kathy feels proud and positive about where her efforts have led her. As she looks back over her ten years in business, she has crossed many hurdles but "stayed the course." Office Remedies has come a long way from its humble beginnings as "a bootstrap operation with no formal financial or consulting support." Kathy still has the flexibility she needs to attend a school function or stay home with a sick child. She can see her children off to school in the morning and meet them at the bus in the afternoon. She's helping many other moms achieve a work-family balance that is manageable, and she meets a good-sized payroll every month.

Growth for Kathy has been challenging, overwhelming at times, but ultimately the next logical step for her thriving business. She's made it work—on her terms.

But sometimes forging ahead *isn't* the right move.

Tina Johnson admits that the steady growth of her events-planning and management business, Johnson Promotions, Inc., has taken its toll in other areas of her life. It hasn't always been easy to juggle the needs of a growing family with the increasingly burdensome demands of her seven-year-old business, and Tina eventually found it necessary to do some serious soul-searching about the future and the role the business would play in her life.

Johnson Promotions started out as a one-woman operation (helped by husband Andy) staging two smallish family-oriented events each year on a shoestring budget. These family "expos" were designed to help parents discover and locate services, resources, and products that would make parenting easier—a "one-stop information-shopping" experience. Tina, herself a mother of four young boys, was also pleased to provide a forum for other home-based moms to exhibit and promote their businesses.

Eventually, Tina consolidated the two shows into one large annual event, held each fall. But by then she wasn't the only business in the area offering this type of show, so the stakes were getting higher. The competition (which was often better funded than Tina's business) meant that Tina's show had to get bigger, better, and longer (two to three days instead of one) every year and be able to attract several major corporate sponsors in order to survive. Tina couldn't do all this alone, and so she soon found her hands full with employees, seasonal temporary staff to "man" the shows, leased office space, and a rapidly escalating budget. She was also increasingly busy with the consulting business that evolved as other organizations, impressed with her shows, approached her to manage their events. As if that weren't enough, Tina decided to reinforce her hands-on experience by attending night school to earn a diploma.

Meanwhile, at home she had four growing boys—all under the age of ten—and found herself beginning to question the way things were going.

Tina's strong commitment to building her business kept her going through many crises and difficult moments, but she was beginning

What If You Relocate?

Your business is finally up and running, you've found a great balance between family and business time, and your spouse comes home one day with good news—and bad news. The good news is that he's been offered a promotion. The bad news? If he accepts the job, you and your family will have to relocate. Can you take your business with you?

As long as your business isn't a strictly local, community-oriented business, the answer is most definitely yes. But even if you do have to start over, you can bring along all your expertise, knowledge, and business savvy, which will make starting up much easier the second time around. Here are some tips:

- *Plan ahead.* Research the business climate in your new location by talking to local realtors and calling the chamber of commerce. Pick up a copy of the local yellow pages and some community publications to get a feel for the place and check on the competition in town.

- *Give yourself time to settle in.* Don't try to do too much until you have settled down in the new home and the children are used to their new schools or play groups.

- *Feel confident about your future.* Unless you are trying to relocate a snow-shoveling service from Montana to Mississippi, there's no reason why you can't replicate your earlier success.

- *Dive in enthusiastically.* Join networking groups and other organizations in your new town. Announce your new business to the press. (See our section on publicity in Phase III.) In fact, do everything you did the first time around, only better!

to realize that any future growth would be at the expense of her family. She knew that in order to grow the business, her next steps would include taking the expo "on the road" to other large cities and/or bidding on more projects to increase her consulting revenue. But to make either move meant that Tina would have even less time to devote to the family—an unacceptable outcome. So after weighing all the options, Tina decided to put the brakes on the business and reconfigure her involvement so that it conflicted less with her role as mom and could better accommodate the needs of her family.

Fortunately, although she began her business with no planning or events-management experience—just a strong desire to build a community-oriented business that would help young families—she has parlayed her experience into an active, financially rewarding consulting practice which she is keeping to a manageable level. She has turned down opportunities to bid on projects that would be too time-consuming and is preparing to move out of the office space that she leased and back to her home office.

Tina knows that within five years she will be in a very different position in her personal life, and she can pick up the pace then. For now, though, she says, "I think that running a business makes me a better role model and a better mother to the boys, but I've learned to prioritize and find the balance. No amount of money is going to give me more time, and that's what I need right now."

And Hubby Makes Two?

What if your husband wants to join you in your business? Can it work? Will your marriage survive it? It's a situation that has worked well for Karen and Ed Lee.

Ed had always been supportive and enthusiastic about Technical Resources, the high-tech recruiting firm Karen started in 1990. They had planned right from the start that Ed would join the business as soon as it could support them both and their two sons. In 1991, Ed left his job and joined Karen full-time. Both felt confident that as a couple they were well equipped to weather the ups and downs of joint entrepreneurship. They attribute this in part to three factors: their friendship and genuine enjoyment of each other's company; respect for the other's talents, abilities, and methods (even when they differ!); and a willingness to compromise when necessary. The Lees also "fight fair," says Karen, who adds, "We're not dirty fighters; we respect each other when we fight. I think the reason we *can* work together is because we've always been able to resolve things."

Like other couples who have made a home-based business work, Ed and Karen particularly relish the flexibility and freedom their lifestyle has brought, whether it's taking time to enjoy lunch together every day or appreciating extra family time with their three children. It has also allowed Karen to back off the business for a time during her pregnancies and while they designed and built their "dream house" in the country, which also gave them a spacious basement office.

If you and your spouse are seriously considering joining forces, here are some suggestions that will help promote harmony in the office—and the bedroom!

- Make sure your financial situation is secure. Financial pressure has been the ruin of many good relationships, and that's without the additional stress of working together!

- Analyze each other's strengths and talents and divide the workload accordingly. Spend some time discussing and figuring out how to channel the mix of strengths appropriately to benefit your business.

- Be tolerant of each other's differences in temperament and work style. Remember, there's more than one way to skin a cat, and if your partner gets results, does it matter how he or she got there?

- Be in synch with your vision for the business. It's no good wanting to build a Fortune 500 if your spouse's goal is a small community-oriented business that pays the bills but leaves lots of family time. Review your goals together regularly to make sure you both still share the same vision.

- Before you decide to work together, hash out a conflict-resolution plan so that you don't have to "fight dirty." You will undoubtedly have conflicts, and if you don't resolve them as they arise, it's not only bad for business, it could be fatal for your relationship.

■ While you're divvying up business-related chores, spend some time on how you'll manage your domestic responsibilities, too. Who will stop work to help the children with homework? Who will cook dinner and do the laundry? Who will run the vacuum and get the baby's bottle? The more you can organize and assign before you start, the fewer problems you will have, because you will both have established expectations.

■ Make a rule to have at least one "no-business-talk-allowed" evening each week. Try to get out of the house with or without the children and focus on anything and everything but business-related things!

■ Schedule time apart from each other. Inevitably, when you live, work, and parent together, there will be times when you need to take a break. Make sure you are each involved in some activities that you enjoy independently.

■ Be prepared to apologize if you've made a mistake and congratulate your partner for a job well done.

Final Thoughts

American writer Lisa Alther once said, "Any mother could perform the jobs of several air traffic controllers with ease." Most of us do that day in and day out as we practice the juggling feat known as motherhood. Now, after having read this book, you're ready to add yet another ball to your act—a new business.

We hope that the ideas, suggestions, and experiences of other moms in this book have helped put you on a firm footing as you begin your adventure. We encourage you to refer to these pages often and feel a little more inspired and reassured each time you pick it up. When your client base is low, reread our marketing section and try something new to attract new clientele. When you feel your plate is way too full and you might just buckle under the weight of it all, reread our time-management section and ask yourself what you could be doing to make your hectic life a little less hectic.

You will learn a great deal as a new business owner, and it will sometimes test the limits of your patience. Growing a business isn't all that different from raising a child; the minute you think you have it "figured out," something will change, and it's back to the drawing board. You will make good decisions and bad decisions, and you will learn from both and quickly find out that experience is absolutely the best teacher.

You may even find that the business idea you began with is not the business you actually end up with at all. And that's okay. The market may not be ready for you yet, your needs and interests may change, or you might just conclude that you picked the wrong thing. But your experience will be your stepping-stone to future success. You'll revamp your initial business or start a whole new business using the skills you learned from developing the old.

We hope that with this book at your side you'll go forward, reassured by the knowledge that many of us have walked the same path and faced the same challenges. And, like every true entrepreneur, you won't be afraid to use disappointment as your incentive to beat the odds.

When you opened this book, you were looking for a way back home, because that's where you want to be for now. From these pages you have learned how to build a business, make time for it in your busy life, and use marketing to make it grow. You have begun to see your role as Mom in a whole new light, and your family is getting to know a different side of you as they watch you shuttle deftly from home to business and back again.

You have already made significant progress, cleared many hurdles, and you're ready to embark on the next chapter. The rest, we hope, will be child's play!

From two mothers to another: Good luck!

Checklist for Phase III

☐ I have identified my target market as follows:

_____

_____

_____

☐ I have researched my competition and can improve on their product or service in the following ways:

_____

_____

_____

☐ I have thought about ways to expand my market in the future as follows:

_____

_____

_____

☐ I understand the process of setting marketing objectives and have identified the following as marketing objectives I can strive for:

_____

_____

_____

☐ I know how to devise a plan to meet my marketing objectives.

☐ I have read through the "Marketing Tools" section and feel that the following tools will work best for my business:

_____

_____

_____

☐ I plan to use the media to my advantage in the following ways:

_____

_____

_____

_____

☐ I think the following charitable activities would work well for my business:

_____

_____

_____

_____

☐ I know I can give my clients the "personal touch" and maintain a positive business image by doing the following on a regular basis:

_____

_____

_____

☐ I think I can implement as least five marketing tools on a regular basis, such as:

☐ I've thought about the consequences of growing too fast and realize that I need to be aware of this as I build my business.

Resources

One thing you won't be short of when starting a home-based business is resource information—books, publications, newsletters, online publications, organizations; the list goes on and on! Rather than list everything we could possibly find here and run the risk that the information would have changed by the time you are reading this book, we've selected a few of our favorite resources to include. For further information or help locating more resources,

- Check your local library or bookstore listings under home-based business, business for women, entrepreneurship, or the specific topic you need help with, such as marketing, publicity, business accounting, etc.
- Do an online search under home-based business; you'll either be thrilled or horrified by the pages of information you receive!

Organizations

American Association of Home Based Businesses   (202) 310-3130
P.O. Box 10023, Rockville, MD 20849
A national, nonprofit association with chapters and networking groups in many states. Send self-addressed stamped envelope for tip sheet on starting a home-based business.

MATCH (Mothers' Access to Careers at Home)   (703) 205-9664
P.O. Box 123, Annandale, VA 22003
Nonprofit organization offering support, networking, and ad-

vocacy for mothers who work from home. Currently forming chapters. Call for further information.

Magazines, Periodicals, Newsletters

Home Office Computing magazine
  The name is a bit of a misnomer. Good basic coverage of many aspects of working from home.

The Art of Self-Promotion by Ilise Benun
(800) 737-0783. Fax (201) 222-2494. P. O. Box 23, Hoboken, NJ 07030.
  Quarterly newsletter filled with practical marketing tips for self-employed professionals and entrepreneurs.

Welcome Home
8310A Old Courthouse Road, Vienna, VA 22182. (800) 783-4666.
  Monthly publication by mothers at home for mothers at home. Great validation if you're new to being home.

Online Publications

Business at Home
  http://www.gohome.com. Online publication for home-based businesses.

Work At Home Moms
  http://www.WAHM.com. Written especially for moms with links to other good sites.

Books

Working From Home
  By Paul and Sarah Edwards (Jeremy P. Tarcher/Putnam, 1994). Probably the best, most comprehensive book on working from home, though it won't help you much with your family/business mix.

Staying Home: From Full-Time Professional to Full-Time Parent
  By Darcie Sanders and Martha Bullen (Little, Brown, 1992). This

book can help you survive the "transition" when you first come home.

Mothering the New Mother

By Sally Placksin (Newmarket Press, 1994). Subtitled "Your Postpartum Resource Companion," Placksin's book will help any new mom through the postpartum period.

How to Succeed On Your Own

By Karin Abarbanel (Henry Holt, 1994). Although not specifically geared to moms, features interesting stories of women entrepreneurs making the switch from employee to entrepreneur.

Blow Your Own Horn

By Jeffrey P. Davidson (Berkeley, 1991). Strategies for making yourself and your business visible and newsworthy.

30 Day Gourmet

By Nanci Slagle and Tara Wohlenhaus. Step-by-step format that walks the family cook through planning, shopping, and preparing foods for the freezer. $25 + shipping and handling. Call (1-888) 803-5604 or (1-317) 852-8537 or contact website http://www.30DayGourmet.com for ordering information.

Let us know how you are doing by visiting our website on the Internet at Moneymakingmoms.com or write to us at Moneymaking Moms, P.O. Box 2455, Manassas, Virginia, 20108.

Acknowledgments

It isn't possible to thank everyone who contributed in some way to this book. So many wonderful individuals have affected our thoughts, validated our choices, and mentored and supported us on our journey through motherhood and home-based business.

First and foremost, thanks to our families, who worked through the wrinkles as we did. Our husbands, Renny Hull and John Wallace, stepped in and did what had to be done as we raced from kitchen to computer to car pool and back again. Our children learned to understand that although they were the motivation behind this book, that role came with a certain responsibility—to let Mom work! Thanks to all eight of you.

We both want to thank our parents, Tom and Joy Williams and Taj and Ingrid Farouki, for raising us to make good choices, to dare to be different, and for showing us how to love our children.

This project may never have materialized if not for the foresight of Lisa Kaufman, formerly of Carol Publishing Group, who saw the potential in a book that addressed the needs of moms who wanted to work from home. Our thanks, too, to our editor, Carrie Nichols Cantor, who took the baton, ran with it, and through her efforts made *Moneymaking Moms* a better book.

We must also thank Jane Jordan Browne, our agent, who believed in the merits of this project and guided us through the early stages of the book.

Finally, our thanks to the most important contributors to this book—the mothers who shared their ideas, experiences, problems, and wisdom with us. Their ability to juggle family, business, and other activities on a daily basis is testimony to the amazing dexterity that motherhood somehow endows. We are proud to be in their company.

Index